A FAMILY LIFE
1939–45

A FAMILY LIFE
1939–45

a journal by

KATHARINE MOORE

ALLISON & BUSBY
Published by W. H. Allen & Co. Plc

An Allison & Busby book
Published in 1989 by
W. H. Allen & Co. Plc
Sekforde House 175/9 St John Street
London EC1V 4LL

Phototypeset in Plantin by Input Typesetting Ltd, London
Printed and bound in Great Britain by
Mackays of Chatham PLC, Chatham, Kent

ISBN 0 85031 935 8

A FAMILY LIFE
1939–45

1939

[*In January 1939 we were living in one of a row of eighteenth-century houses in Upper High Street, Sevenoaks. It was a pleasant, small house, rented from fierce old Mrs Constant who owned the row and herself occupied the lovely Queen Anne house a few doors away, once the coaching inn where Jane Austen had stayed. We had two rooms on each of the three floors and a long narrow garden behind, bordering on Knole Park. My two children, Christopher and Jane (twins) were fifteen: Chris a day boy at Sevenoaks School and Jane, who had been at St Christopher's, Letchworth, was now working at home for her School Certificate (i.e. 'O' levels), though she was going back to St Christopher's to take it. My two elder stepdaughters were both recently married, Madeleine to Leslie Bromford (Bunny), a farmer in Hampshire, and Judith to Richard Hull, an Oxford don. The youngest, Anthea, was at Reading University. My husband, Dr Harold Moore, was Director of the Non-Ferrous Research Association in London.*

I began the year with two visits, first to Madeleine who was not well and needing cheering up and then on the way home to my Oxford friend, Evelyn Tatham at her home Northcourt House, Abingdon.]

JANUARY 11TH

At Northcourt once more. When I came here first 20 years ago I thought it the nicest house I had ever known, but I accepted it all as simply existing – immutable and everlasting. Now it has all the poignancy of an uneasy survival. Mean little houses have sprung up all around in what used to be open fields and there is an aerodrome only a mile away which has driven John Masefield from Boars Hill. The house stands up among the housing estate, a relic of a past culture. I expect the Tathams are the last family that will ever live here; when Mrs Tatham dies it will be pulled down or turned into an institution of some sort. [*Actually it was run as a school by Evelyn Tatham till she died in 1974 and then was turned into flats.*] Meanwhile I still think it a lovely place and the old schoolroom the pleasantest room in the world.

JANUARY 13TH

The weather is so fine, I got my first impression of warm sun this year and found myself thinking 'how lovely spring and summer will be' and then came the usual reservation: 'if there is no war', and curiously enough I got this first intimation of spring in the middle of the horrid little new housing estate bordering on Northcourt. Suddenly the sun on the bricks seemed a lovely thing and I felt that if I owned one of those little houses I should feel proud of it and come to the door in the sunshine loving it, or if I were seeing it perhaps for the first time, after being shut away by illness, it wouldn't look ugly or mean at all. Home tomorrow to telephone and jobs!

JANUARY 18TH
Interviewed Mr W. of Winchester House Preparatory
School about our refugee boy – a kind, little man, obviously rather a snob but the school seemed nice and he
will take Christoph Heu at reduced fees. At six went to
the Committee, Miss Ramsay is very keen to collect
funds to send Jewish refugee children to the Caldicott
Community because the schools are so overcrowded
here. After supper unwisely talked about international
affairs with H which made me sleepless and miserable –
to think about them *at all* is like falling into a nightmare
from normal waking life. Jane has done a picture of
the country round Madeleine's Farm, which I think
fascinating. She would not let me have it though. Am
reading Bertrand Russell's *Power*.

JANUARY 22ND
Ena, our Danish help, while making the beds with me,
said that in a Danish paper the U.S.A. Ambassador is
reported as saying that war is inevitable this spring. To
tea with the Cummings family. [*My sister was married to
H. R. Cummings, the brother of A. J. Cummings of the
News Chronicle, and of Bruce Cummings alias 'Barbellion'
('Journal of a Disappointed Man')*] Hal arrived from
Geneva during tea, fairly cheerful and full of stories of
Germany being in a bad way.

JANUARY 25TH
Snow again. Met E at T. Wells. [*Evelyn Tatham was
now HM of a private school at Crowborough.*] She has

taken in a new Austrian refugee child at her school and has now quite a number. On the way home the bus stopped at Riverhill and on investigation there were found to be about 22 lorries and 10 other vehicles stranded all over the road so another woman and I decided to walk home. The going was very wet and sloshy, but the air was lovely and the trees exquisite. The stranger was one of those lonely but affluent females that often haunt seaside resorts. This one was staying at a nursing home in Sevenoaks because she liked the district, though she complained of Knole Park being draughty!

JANUARY 26TH

Barcelona fallen. Felt depressed all day. Edward Grubb has died. [*He was a notable Friend, a member of Letchworth Meeting and was very kind to me there when Chris was run over by a van and in hospital with a broken arm and leg.*]

JANUARY 27TH

To London to the morning session at Friends' House on Economics and Peace. Speech on soil nutrition which seemed a little off the point, but was interesting. Lunch with H who told me that the trip to America was definitely off. In spite of fearing much worse things than this comparably trivial news, I had a fit of longing, not so much for this five weeks' luxury and travel with H as for a world in which such a thing was still possible. I must have more courage. Edward Grubb once quoted to me Pascal's 'Thou woudst not seek God if thou hadst not already found him.' I wish I could feel that true but I feel I only seek Him because I can't bear life without a source of spiritual strength and so it seems to me a weakness, not a sign of grace.

Have finished Bertrand Russell's 'Power'. He convinces me of the danger of any other form of government than a democracy in spite of its defects. He believes that freedom and democracy must win in the end – but meanwhile?? He says the four most powerful people in history were Christ, Buddha, Galileo and Pythagoras – Chris, when I asked him to guess, said the first three straight away, but substituted Aristotle for Pythagoras.

JANUARY 30TH

To Crouch to Ellen Easdale for lunch. She looked exquisite as usual – her hair tied up on top with a narrow red ribbon and a long string of amber beads. She is an extraordinary mixture of wisdom and foolishness – wisdom on the necessity of acceptance of life in its fullest extent and in her general attitude to war, in her acute literary appreciation, and foolishness in solemn assurance that because she had heard of the birth of various girl babies lately, it was a sure sign that there would be no war! On the whole though the wisdom wins and her charm never fails.

The drive back was so pretty; Seal Chart covered with bright snow and little beech trees, still flaunting their red-brown leaves, sticking up out of it, and the bracken exactly the same colour as the beeches, also poking up out of the whiteness. The bark of the birch trees repeated the black-and-white patchiness of the earth beneath.

A tea party at Miss Drummond's, all the old aristocrats of Sevenoaks there, remembering the rows of maidservants from Knole in their little round bonnets in the front pews of St Nicholas every morning and Pepita's daughter driving to the R.C. Church and the farmhouses in the lower High Street. Conversation at tea: 'Of course what I say is England always has the man for the hour. A year or so ago we knew nothing about Mr Chamberlain and now here he is – the greatest man in the world!'

Miss Drummond asked me if I had seen the picture of Magnolia, the prize black heifer at the Fatstock Show. I had not. She had written four letters to protest against Magnolia having been sold to a butcher without success, but the owner, Lady H, had asked her to go and see her prize herd. Lovely tea and beautiful china. Reading *The Newcomes* at night as a soporific. Trying to find homes for two charming Viennese children whose photographs have been sent to me.

FEBRUARY
Liberal lunch to hear Helen Simpson speak, an appallingly competent woman.

FEBRUARY 9TH & 10TH
Reading Gibbons' *Decline and Fall* with Jane. An advert of Cook's Tours focused my longing for travel again. Family problems are converging. Poor Jimmy's letter this morning makes me feel I must go to Reading at

once to try and do what I can for him. Anthea seems to be breaking his heart (he is such a nice boy) and Madeleine writes that she is still not well and wants to come here from Wednesday to Sunday. We are also having to fetch our refugee boy Christoph Heu on Saturday and have heard that he is older than we thought. Meanwhile Mrs Fenn has flu which leaves extra Peace work to be done. The U.D.C. [*Urban District Council*] write for volunteers for evacuation work etc. etc. I also try to get on with Jane's lessons. I met Evelyn Harvey today who has almost ceased to be a personality – she is so immersed in refugee affairs and so worn out by them.

FEBRUARY 20TH

We went to fetch Christoph Heu from Haywards Heath but brought back his brother Berti aged 11 instead. C is very big and mature for his age (14) and would not fit into Winchester House School at all. He is to go to one of the Friend's schools. Berti is settling down with us quite well. Their father is a well-known Austrian sculptor married to a Jew and therefore given the option of abandoning her or leaving the country. They have very little in the way of belongings but are thankful to get out and are being looked after by friends in Yorkshire.

Austrian Party at the Chantry. [*The Chantry was the HQ of a religious order in Sevenoaks.*] Talked English history with the Bergsons [*refugees from Vienna*] who afterwards said the evening made them feel civilized again.

MARCH

To Madeleine at Tuften Warren. [*This was the spacious and beautiful farm in Hampshire belonging to Madeleine's husband – one of a famous farming family.*] Bunny's brother staying here, he is like a big, very good natured dog. He and Bunny don't read but they are very interesting on country lore. He is very pleased that the rooks are building in the trees in front of the Farm. He says his father used to try to attract the rooks to his farm at Evesham by lashing old nests and calves' quarters onto the trees. Young rooks have to build nests for their elders for two years.

APRIL 3RD

A fortnight of fear and depression over the international situation. Hitler's seizure of Prague means that his word can no longer be relied on and therefore he can no longer be negotiated with – also that he means to dominate Europe and not just to unite German peoples. Now all hopes are at an end and one is driven to live from day to day clinging to three possibilities, first that a strong combination of force against Hitler may make him stop, secondly that he or Mussolini may die, or lastly that America may make a definite proclamation against them. How many people now must be praying for Hitler's death. Even sweet, dear, little Quaker Mrs Bartholomew said she did not think it could be wrong to do so.

I would give much to think that war is now justified and of use. To be a pacifist and have to support a war one doesn't believe in is unbearable. I catch myself hoping I am wrong and that war *would* save freedom and democ-

racy, but yet I can't somehow believe that modern warfare can bring anything but chaos and suffering and such
bitterness that a lasting peace could *not* follow – look at
the last war! It still seems to me that passive resistance
to evil carried out on a large scale would bring about a
more lasting regeneration in spite of terrible suffering.
But as there isn't the slightest hope of the nation adopt-
ing such a policy, what now? Even if we frighten off
Hitler for the time being it would only be temporary,
and I can't help feeling that England is right to promise
help to Poland in the case of aggression. If only we could
combine effectively now with America and Russia's help.

The reactions of my friends during this fortnight are
various. E has been very depressed, N feels that life has
become more vivid and significant under the threat,
G.H. and E.M.T. more convincingly pacifist, and K,
like myself, is haunted by a nightmare feeling of unre-
ality. H is always calm for which I am generally grateful
though occasionally it exasperates me. Once I said to
him: 'I believe if a bomb dropped on me and the children
in the garden you'd only say 'how interesting'. He said,
'No, I wouldn't, but it would be,' and then of course I
laughed and felt better. How lucky to have a husband
who can nearly always make me laugh. Our little refugee
boy Berti Heu is rather sweet. He is imaginative and
sensitive but very excitable and finds it difficult to
concentrate.

APRIL 5TH
Drove to see Mother and Dad; both very well. Dad will
not discuss politics which means that they are too bad
for his optimistic nature to face.

The children are both in Scotland. I missed them terribly at first, but now enjoy more leisure and especially more time with H alone. He is being delightful. We have finished reading together *My Country and My People*. Points that struck me about the Chinese as illustrated by this book are: importance of calligraphy as a form of art and of rhythm in painting, inspiration from nature rather than people and the sanity of these artists! They are quite soothing to read about because of this balance.

APRIL 7TH – 12TH

At Walkhurst, Benenden. The children from the farm cottage had filled the house full of flowers for us – wallflowers in the old brown jug – daffodils in the green one and an egg cup full of white violets. Long walk with H – a blue haze over the marshes, peewits calling everywhere, enormous primroses in the lanes. At night, saw primroses everywhere when I shut my eyes. Perkin, our white cat, saw an adder in the garden among the dead leaves, it very much surprised him. They have nearly finished stringing the hop garden.

[*Besides the home in Sevenoaks we had rented Walkhurst, a small seventeenth-century farmhouse at Benenden with a view to ultimately retiring there and meanwhile we used it for a retreat whenever we could. It was a great refreshment to us both.*]

APRIL 12TH

Back in Sevenoaks. At supper, Miss Bridge from the Chantry called about refugee business. She always looks dignified and rather noble, just as the head of a religious order ought to look, but she has a great sense of humour and is not a saint. Our wireless returned from the shop; the man bringing it said he might be called up in the Army Reserve tomorrow.

APRIL 20TH – 24TH

To Stratford with Evelyn, but she had to go home the next day as her mother wasn't well and I was alone at the guest house, but resolved to make contact with some other guest and chose the young man whose shoes left outside his bedroom door had looked interesting. We exchanged views over 'Twelfth Night' at breakfast and he invited me to stand by his flag at the Shakespeare birthday celebration. (He had been a member of the Birmingham Rep).

As we were talking a little man suddenly burst into the room and began to tell us about a book he had just found that proved that Jesus had lived in England for seven years and built the first Church at Glastonbury.

'How does your book prove it?' 'Well, he was a carpenter, wasn't he? He lived at Glastonbury with Joseph of Arimathea – why, one of our poets tells us as plain as can be: 'And did those feet in Ancient Time walk upon England's pastures green.' You believe all the lies they tell you in the newspaper – I believe in tradition that can't lie and comes down to us in spite of lies.'

Clive (the name of my new friend) calmed him down

and we went out together to the flag raising. His flag was at the bottom of the street. The Czech flag (to be raised by refugees) was next. Great excitement was caused by the German flag falling to the ground, but I missed seeing this, being much interested in the Japanese who couldn't get his flag to work at all. It is curious that these two flags, the German and the Japanese, were the only ones that came to grief. A policeman was stationed by the German flag for the rest of the day. After the ceremony the flag raisers formed into a procession. I had no right at all to be in this procession of international dignitaries in silk hats with huge laurel wreaths and bouquets of roses. I happened to have a green check silk handkerchief with me which I tied round my head and I carried the humble bunch of daffodils I had hastily bought on the way. We proceeded slowly through the town watched by the crowds and were received at Shakespeare's birthplace, where I think I was taken for a distinguished foreigner, as a gentleman receiving us explained to me carefully and most kindly the known facts about Shakespeare's life. Then we went to the church and laid our flowers on the tomb. It was all very pleasant and informal, and yet gracious in the best English tradition. My friend, who was very charming, had lived in Russia as a child. He invited me to a drink before the theatre tonight. I enjoyed my morning thoroughly and very much enjoyed the 'Comedy of Errors' that evening which was done to Handel's music rather like a Russian ballet.

APRIL 28TH

Refugee Committee – I fear I have let myself in for domestic agency work.

MAY 12TH

To Jordans [*the historic Quaker Meeting House in Bucks*] with H for the Unity Group Meetings [*of scientists and philosophers which included several interesting people*]. Herbert Samuel, full of vitality still, has a very pleasing voice and delivery. He wants a synthesis of philosophy and religion – morals and ethics to be the business of philosophy and emotion to be dealt with by religion. John Harvey – jolly, sincere and kind. Dorothy Emmett – donnish, very clever and a bit snubbing. Hawton, an enthusiastic but not aggressive communist, wistfully repudiating religion but looking forward radiantly to a communist Europe following a short war.

Mr and Mrs Salamon, she a handsome woman looking after herself well in the way of comfortable chairs, extra fruit, electric fires etc. He, an immense fair man, very hostile to religion, obsessed by potato research (religion in his eyes is a virus comparable to the potato virus!).

Old Muirhead, like a slender walrus, talking of 'our young optimists'.

Marvin, a benevolent but most positive Positivist, a typical nineteenth-century survival.

By far the most interesting speaker was John Macmurray. He said that this was not a scientific age in the true sense, but an age of technology. How we can *use* the world has become the dominant question – we have lost sight of ends and see only means. Appeasement good in its intentions but not possible to fit into facts. All that he said made sense to me. Nearly everyone here seems to be either a Scot or a Jew.

JUNE 6TH

Lovely day for the Party [*the Peace Party at the Chantry, which I had helped to organize*]. Went there in good time but worried that there was no word about the children and neither the chairs nor the china had come; however all arrived eventually and all went well except that I called Miss Bridge Miss Church by mistake in my speech! The Basque children were enchanting, very happy and unselfconscious, their dancing so graceful and looking lovely against the background of the Chantry garden. Dr Bergsen for the refugees thanked us for 'giving back the worst loss, the loss of faith in human nature'. The day ended happily and I hope gave a good deal of enjoyment though it may not have spread pacifism!

JUNE 21ST

A cold wet morning, so put on far too many clothes, for when Jane and I got to London the sun came out and it got thundery and hot. Jane was miserable because owing to the wet morning she had missed wearing her new sailor hat. But we found comfort and joy in the National Gallery. Then I saw her off to Letchworth with a sinking heart. The children are so nice, pleasant and sensible that I enjoy their company immensely and miss them very much when they are away.

JUNE 22ND

To poor Madeleine in hospital and stayed with her till they came to get her ready for the operation. She was frightened and miserable, but charming to the nurse. I said 'I am sure you will be all right'. M (smiling up at the nurse) 'Of *course* I shall be when everyone takes such good care of me.' I believe she would take the trouble to be charming to the executioner if she were being beheaded. Gracie Fields is in the same hospital and the landing outside her room is a mass of flowers.

JUNE 24TH

To Benenden, stopping to get flour at Cranbook Mill. Curiously happy here as always.

JUNE 28TH

Hal, my brother-in-law, came to stay. He told me of a German officer who had lunched with him and with Admiral Godfrey who said the German people are so deafened by propaganda that they take no notice of words any more – only of deeds, that Hitler is not influenced by Ribbentrop or indeed by anyone, and that he hoped that he (the officer) could return to Germany and say that this country was so well prepared that he could not advise war. Hilarious breakfast with Chris singing the school song. Ellen Easdale rang me up: 'My dear, say what you will the devil is abroad and he waits to see where he can nip in and there he goes. I can't bear it!' and a lot more about God and the state of the universe and the devil till the butcher hammering on the door put a stop to it.

JULY 9TH

Workmen have begun to repair the roof and woken me up this morning by throwing tiles about. Had to dress with shutters closed. At breakfast found we had run out of bread *and* cereal. Tried to settle down to give Jane her last coaching before the exam, but interruptions incessant – Mrs Fenn on getting over another married couple from Austria, Dr J. N. calling, and Ellen Easdale again full of an iniquitous article in the *Telegraph* against the P.P.U. [*Peace Pledge Union*] Promised her to write to Civil Liberties about it. G. rang to say she was bringing a friend to tea but mercifully she arrived alone. She was writing a lecture on vegetables and wanted to try it out on me. Some refugees called wanting help to get a couple out from Prague – took particulars. Chris came home – I don't think there will be enough supper for everyone!

Berti arrived very late from school with 3 frogs in a jar for which he wanted an immediate pool. Promised him pool after supper, gave him his supper and sent him to bed, but he came down again to tell me Mr Wilson had slippered him and it was unfair and only because he wasn't an English boy (quite untrue of course). I tried to confute this and to comfort, sympathize and inspire him to better behaviour, and tucked him up again.

H came home and I gave him his supper while G read me her lecture. Sent Chris to steal cement from the workman's pile next door to make the pond for the frogs. Sat down to prepare Jane's history lesson. 11.30 went to bed. H came up but I got him to go down again to make a hole in the top of the jar in case the frogs smothered in the night – the pond isn't ready yet! A full day.

JULY 13TH

Anthea brought home Gordon Roxburgh whom she wants to marry in the autumn. I felt just like Lady Stavely in Trollope's *Orley Farm*, as I am so fond of poor Jimmy, and I saw it was no good when I went down to Reading. Gordon R. looks like Mephistopheles. Anthea was very appealing and young. I *hope* it's all right.

JULY 29TH – 31ST

School end of term events. Sevenoaks School concert – Chris playing a piano concerto for 2 pianos with his friend Stubbs. He forgot his music, but with his usual friendly unselfconsciousness just smiled at the audience and said, 'Sorry, shan't be a minute,' and fetched it. Berti's school sports next day. It poured with rain most of the time. Mrs Wilson Senior made her speech from under an umbrella.

'I hope all you dear boys will go on doing better and better in every way and whatever you do always remember all through your lives "to play up, play up and play the game" and I can't say more than that.' Then, also ignoring the pouring rain, a handsome bland looking clergyman rose to thank Mrs W for her speech and the school for existing and to shame his young son by quoting a howler of his before the assembled company. Berti was worn out by his excitement but thank goodness had won the three-legged race and the sack race!

Mr and Mrs Ulrich (refugees) came to coffee in the evening – rather frightening – he so clever and she so handsome; however they stayed till past eleven. They were very complimentary about English education – its balance and fairness etc. Chris off to the Friends Summer School in Normandy and Jane to Judith at Oxford and Berti to visit his parents in Yorkshire, so the house seems very empty and quiet.

AUGUST 5TH
[At Hodcombe, the Sussex home of my parents]
Jane and I spent the day at Brighton. In 'The Lanes' was pleased to find a facsimile of my Staffordshire pottery figure, Will Watch, for which I had given 7/6d at Sevenoaks priced at two guineas here. Learnt that he was a famous smuggler whose headquarters was at Birling Gap. Tea with Aunt Aida after having had enormous ices in Regency Square. Aunty Aida said Eastbourne was too respectable for her – she liked a little wickedness and vulgarity. Dad can't believe this and is trying to get her to move to Eastbourne to be nearer him. Chris arrived very late, having missed his train and come to the end of his money, but he has obviously had a wonderful time.

1939

AUGUST 8TH

H here for weekend. He took Mother, Jane and myself to Jevingdon to sketch. A perfect evening, the corn stooks shining gold in the evening light. Mother and Jane talked incessantly while they sketched. Mother would not let us look at hers and tore it up, Jane did a good strong picture – mine feeble as usual. We all enjoyed ourselves and each other thoroughly. Felt happier because there is talk of a five power international conference. The garden is so lovely now – fuchsias against deep blue sky, phlox and lavender fully out and masses of verbena, sun warmer, gooseberry in profusion. Hated leaving.

AUGUST 16TH – 24TH

At Abingdon with the Tathams [*to be near Judith who was expecting her baby*]. A dreadful time of national suspense. Took Judith to the Acland Nursing Home. Richard went off on a climbing holiday (typical!) Judith said 'Goodbye – have a good holiday.' He said, 'Goodbye have a good baby!' She says she'd rather have him out of the way. But still! The baby, Rachel Margaret, arrived on the 20th. I saw them both the next day – it was a relief to visit them and to talk to Judith who must not be worried by the war situation.

AUGUST 22ND

German–Russian pact signed. At first I thought no war would now be possible as we should not be strong enough to oppose the joint force and, though utterly miserable at what looks a triumph for Hitler, yet felt relief that we should escape destruction. But it seems that we are sticking to our pledge to Poland. It is very hard to get through these days. Mr Kennedy (Vicar) takes the same view as I did yesterday – i.e. that we shall not dare to fight. In the bus on the way to Burford [*where I was going to stay with another old Oxford friend*], the country people seemed very depressed. How different from the mood of 1914. I can hardly bear to look at the men bringing in the harvest and to think what happened to their fathers in 'the war to end war' and now may happen to them. There seems no sign of weakening by the government. It is awful to believe them wrong, in fact very hard to be a pacifist. At Burford, Katharine, [*K. M. Briggs, an old Oxford friend, writer and folklorist*] though hating and fearing war, is all for honour etc. I expected this. I slept for scarcely an hour trying to face up to the worst and to find strength and hope. Read Cecil's *Lord Melbourne* some of the night which K had put by my bed.

AUGUST 24TH

Picnicked at Kelmscott by the river – the scent of the water and the meadows so nostalgic of old Oxford days, and the old beautiful house and garden made me ache for love of the English countryside. We inspected the village hall for use for K's Summer Dramatics (will they ever take place?) and then we drove back to Burford. After Supper K read poetry to me and in bed I read *My talks with Dean Spanley* by Lord Dunsaney – a *lovely* book which I must get for Evelyn. News a little better,

Sir N. Henderson coming to England with a message from Hitler.

SATURDAY, AUGUST 26TH

To Cheltenham by bus. [*This was to visit my husband's sisters*]. H arrived at about 8 o'clock. Bliss to see him. News much the same. Georgiana is very pacifist agreeing with me. To Friends Meeting with H. A very small meeting but nice. At night, news slightly more hopeful. The Archbishop of York (Temple) on the wireless told us to love peace and our enemies but to drop bombs on them if necessary. J. B. Priestley in the News Chronicle is so self-righteous about England that one can scarcely bear it.

TUESDAY, AUGUST 28TH

Back to Oxford and had a rebirth of hope when it was obvious that Hitler was still delaying. Met Evelyn for lunch and afterwards bought *Dean Spanley* at Blackwells for her birthday. We sat on the steps of the Bodleian in the sun and argued as to where we had done Schools. [*I said it was in the Divinity School as the school's building was not yet rehabilitated after it had been used as a hospital in the 1914 war. We were probably both right as things were not yet back to normal then*]. A little hope goes to one's head deliriously these days. Afterwards to the Acland to see Judith and the charming baby, and she asked me about the situation as her nurse had told her she might not be able to see after her in the future owing to mobilization. J did not seem too worried though. Home in the evening and phoned to Madeleine to send the twins back from Tufton Warren.

WEDNESDAY, AUGUST 30TH

Breakfast with H in the garden. Everything lovely with the late summer flowers and heavy dew and birds singing. Bought brown paper and drawing pins for possible black out. Many people very hopeful still though. Children arrived home.

THURSDAY, AUGUST 31ST

To Walkhurst with the children and was reading *Dean Spanley* to them when William Moore (no relation!), the Farm foreman came to see me. He wanted to tell me the order for the evacuation of the children from London had been given out on the wireless. Felt very depressed. I shall have to go back to Sevenoaks and the twins begged to go with me so we started after lunch. Moore came over to the car and patted me on the shoulder and with his troubled, kind smile said: 'Don't be too downhearted.' This touched and comforted me.

FRIDAY, SEPTEMBER 1ST

This morning things didn't seem quite so hopeless, as there is again talk of negotiation on Hitler's part with the Poles. We started off for the Farm again and on the way called at Crouch to see Ellen. She met us at the door and said: 'You know we are at war, Germany has marched into Poland.' We went into her sitting room and listened to the news. I then took the children and left them at Benenden and started home again alone.

SATURDAY, SEPTEMBER 2ND

A strange hectic day trying to deal with blackout and getting ready for our evacuees who arrived after lunch. Mrs Shrewsbury, Audrey aged 4 and John aged 10 months. Poor things they seem nice but bewildered. Left with H rather late and it was dark when we reached Brenchley where a policeman stopped us and told us to switch off headlights and shade our side lamps. Just past Goudhurst it became an unbearable strain to drive like that and we switched on the head lamps again, but after another couple of miles a line of soldiers stretched across the road and fiercely told us to switch off at once. 'We are at war now you know.' They were quite kind really though. A mile more of swerving about and we decided to unveil the side lights again. Just afterwards a lorry full of the same soldiers drove past us but did not stop us. At last we reached the Farm.

SUNDAY, SEPTEMBER 3RD

War formally declared by us at 11 o'clock. Immediately after the first air raid warning went off – heard very faintly by us. But it appears that it was a mistake – it was only a harmless neutral plane. Switched on wireless and heard German interference on the air sounding like a harsh maniac babble of disconnected words – a quite terrifying and horrible sound. We are asked not to use cars, phones etc. and feel very cut off but thankful to be all together.

SEPTEMBER AT BENENDEN

Started hop picking and found it soothing though tiring. We began by sharing a bin with an old Cockney woman and her daughter. She was an inveterate old grumbler. 'Nigger's work I call it. I'd give 'im a bit of my mind. Work like a slave all day long and only get a shilling at the end of it – nigger's work that's what it is.' 'Oh stop it Mother!' said the daughter. This went on all the time till we asked Henley (the farmer) to put us among the village people instead and here we had a bin of our own and it was very pleasant except that we simply couldn't keep up at all with the pace of the village pickers. Betty Moore, aged eleven, picked three times more than the four of us in a day. The best time was after H had driven off to work and the children were still in bed, and I was picking alone, soon after 7 a.m. with the sun quietly shining through the white mist and the dew glittering everywhere. But the evenings are lovely too, the oasts and barn brilliant in the evening light and the piled wagon with the horses, Dolly and Flower and young Ted in his blue shirt, all looking as though they had just been created. It's impossible to believe war was declared a few days ago.

OCTOBER 12TH

Life is curiously normal and curiously abnormal. We are used now to the blackout and to evacuees. H keeps his usual hours, food gets a little dearer, income tax is awful. No one knows what is going to happen but people all accommodating themselves to suspense. I am getting more and more deeply involved in refugee work and am now on a committee of refugee welfare with Maude Royden [*ordained woman Minister of the Congregational Church (now United Free Church)*] who is admirable. I feel I am not good at this sort of work but must do it.

OCTOBER 26TH

Our evacuees have gone back to London as nothing seems to be happening. The news continues to be chiefly concerned with shipping attacks, unending speeches on the wireless; Soviet Russia still a dark horse; the Finnish business looks bad. The Turkish pact signed with us has caused jubilation. The plans on foot for moving large populations wholesale are terrifying in their inhumanity. That and the stupidity of our office of Works etc. makes bad reading. Ration cards talked of but not issued yet. Jack Collis' lectures every week are well attended and very inspiring. He was good on Shelley today. 'To a business man time is money – to a creative artist money is Time.' What would Shelley have said to one of these hideous gas masks we are supposed to carry round with us now?' Reading Rosalind Murray's life of her father, Gilbert Murray – [*A Good Pagan's Failure*]. She has too narrow a view of the religious man. Deeds done for humanity's sake are *not* barren as she says and the love of beauty cannot be summarily dismissed. She is a convert to Catholicism which explains a lot.

OCTOBER 29TH

Busy morning, calling and ringing up people about refugees, but off to Benenden in the afternoon – the house warm and welcoming. H played the piano in the evening – the firelight shining on the last dahlias and marigolds in the blue jug. This place is the height of comfort with Mrs Stockwell a refugee from London, in the kitchen looking after us, and *no telephone*. It is very good for H who gets up about two hours later and goes to bed one hour earlier and gets in one good walk.

NOVEMBER 4TH

Met E at National Gallery lunch time concert, [*the war time lunch prom concerts at the N G arranged by Myra Hess*], Solomon playing the Brahms and Debussy did not appeal to me much, but I loved the Beethoven E flat Sonata and there was some nice Chopin. Crowded audience who obviously found it very refreshing. H said that a man got into his train at Knockholt and immediately he had sat down said in a loud clear voice: 'My name is Roberts, last night I had a dream. I dreamed I was in Heaven.' 'They go by opposites,' said the man sitting next to him. 'In Heaven I was singing in a choir. There were hundreds of sopranos, thousands of contraltos – miles of tenors and only one bass. That bass was me. The Archangel Michael was conducting. The enormous choir sang splendidly and I sang as I had never sung before. After we had sung for some time the Archangel Michael stopped us and said, "Mr Roberts, you are singing too loud." ' The train got to Sevenoaks and H had to get out! The trains are quite dark now which is boring. I tried to wind wool on my journey but got in a muddle.

NOVEMBER 6TH

Ramsdale, our old part time gardener and odd job man left today and Chittenden came instead. Both are from the Almshouses. Chittenden is like a little old Dickens character. He was apprenticed to a pastry cook at Rye as a boy. He told H that he and Ramsdale had worked together at Major Fulton's where he had to look after 30 monkeys, 2 lemurs, 1 badger and a holy cow with a hump. He was very afraid of the monkeys. He said when I asked him how he was: 'I'm all right ma'am, except for my rheumatic knee – if it wasn't for that I could jump over the moon. Of course I couldn't really, but that's how I feel, good and spry like.' He told H he couldn't come on Sundays as he liked to go to Chapel then. 'I don't know what you'll think of this Sir, but I'm a lover of Jesus. I don't mean by that that I'm better than other folks. I couldn't have you thinking that.'

To lunch with the Ashbees, Janet and Charles. [*Charles Ashbee – architect and designer, friend of William Morris*] He rather terrifying but friendly. Their big charming room with the piano painted by Burne Jones is now a school for all the evacuated children at Godden Green.

NOVEMBER 9TH

Day began badly, pouring rain and the news of the failure of the bomb *by just 10 minutes*: to blow up Hitler and Hess. My emotional reaction to this irritated H who was probably feeling it just as much but being philosophic and self-controlled, irritated me! Party for refugees weighing on me. Air raid warning went off while I was making the beds. Went in the pouring rain to the Lime Tree Studio to get ready for the party. Guests began to arrive at 3 o'clock and more and more came, seventy-eight refugees altogether. After tea, with much effort, got games going, but once this was done the party ran itself. I must put the girl who wants art classes in touch with Christle Bergson and one difficult case of mother and child must be dealt with, they are unhappy with their present family. Managed to avoid Frau Weiger! Home very tired but pleased at success of the party.

NOVEMBER 10TH

Clearing up after party: took the games back to Mrs Alexander and found her very gloomy – expecting immediate invasion of Holland and quantities of gas blown across to us. It is curious how very pessimistic ordinarily cheerful people become in time of war and vice versa. It is a long time since I heard my sister Dorothy grumble and Ethel Ginsberg is happier than I've known her for years and Mrs H is actually enjoying the war or rather the renewed interest and opportunities it has brought her.

NOVEMBER 11TH

To Madeleine and Bunny with H. The comfort and
space of their house very acceptable and the country
(Hampshire) so restful – no planes! Madeleine looks pale
and tired but hopes very much that she is pregnant.
Bunny has ploughed up about 30 acres of extra land.
We are pleased at the idea of all four of us coming here
for Christmas, but one is rather afraid of looking forward
to anything just now. Came away much refreshed and
weighted with eggs, hare, rabbit and spindleberries – on
the way home, went to National Gallery lunch time
concert (Mozart) and then to contemporary Art at the
Leicester Gallery – a good Meninsky (still life), Vanessa
Bell (carnations against a pink street) – Duncan Grant
(boats.)

NOVEMBER 14TH

Refugee Committee, study circle and wrote letter about
refugees to S. News. I find wireless worrying still. It
disintegrates so; incongruous worlds meet and so experience has the wrong setting. Backgrounds and moods
may not fit at all with a resulting muddle and dishar-
mony; e.g., the announcer's voice coming from an isolated farm or cottage never fails to give me a shock, or
music struggling to be heard against the noise of cars or
church services at meal times.

Listening to Lord Haw Haw [*Lord Haw Haw the name
given to the Irishman Joyce, employed by the Germans to
broadcast 'This is Germany calling the British Isles etc.'*]
broadcasting from Hamburg is frightening with that

nightmare quality of something pretending to be friendly turning into something alien and scornful.

A letter from my dear Nancy B. teasing me for being too much 'the social worker'. I certainly don't do it with my whole heart and therefore not as well as I might, yet I suppose not too badly or I would not be asked to go on. I long for more time to do as I like (i.e. write or laze) and yet I suppose I wouldn't be happy not doing it.

NOVEMBER 19TH

Barbara, my very dear niece and her Edgar to tea. He is very charming – a Jewish refugee. He lays down the law with complete finality but doesn't mind in the least if he is contradicted.

NOVEMBER 20TH

Two refreshing days at the Farm with Jane. Took Mrs Moore a parcel of baby clothes and she seemed very pleased. She has begun her pains; I do hope all goes well and she has a girl, which she wants. Home and went round to the refugee club to arrange music for Thursday. H away for the night. Mrs H gets worse and worse about her refugee boy, Herbert W. How *can* people repudiate their obligations so calmly. Went with Jane to 'Goodbye Mr Chips'. Very good in its way, but *how* sentimental a picture of our great public schools! Anyway Jane and I sat there and wept like anything. Came home and gave Chris a history lesson on Luther and Calvin. I am all for him adding history to his Higher Cert. subjects and as this can't be fitted into his science and maths syllabus at school, he and I are doing it at home when we have time.

NOVEMBER 25TH

Went round to R. Club at 5 o'clock. Very full – cellist from London Philharmonic to play, who arrived very late in corporal's uniform. He played a Jewish hymn, some Bach and Chopin and a Spanish dance: very much appreciated. Fr. W said 'He is playing for my heart'.

Took Jane to Crouch for her French coaching with Frida Earsdale. While she was having it, Benny (our poodle) and I walked to Old Soar, the fields misty and grey. I got some lovely spindleberries and picked up enough apples for a pie tomorrow. We got ourselves covered with burrs which worried Benny rather. He was sick three times in the afternoon, having, I am afraid, eaten some very decomposed rabbit on the walk. Hurried to Chantry prayer circle in the afternoon, but was so sleepy after the long walk that in the warm quiet dusky room I nearly dropped off. This made it embarrassing when Miss Bridge rushed after me to tell me how much more creative my presence made the silence! To Jack Collis' lecture on Carlyle in evening and was cross in the discussion.

DECEMBER 4TH

Very depressed at the news of Russia invading Finland. The war news seems to stretch out into infinity. Chris, Barber, Dinsmore and Stubbs [*all Sevenoaks schoolboys*] played to the refugees in the afternoon. I think they were appreciated. Worried about Fr. Klinge's child, Herbert W and now Frau Flein, who wants to go to Chile and must have £80 to do so. H away for the night.

DECEMBER 15TH

To coffee with the Ulrichs. The other Mrs Ulrich, whose husband had been a judge in Bavaria, had come to see me in the morning to try on my dress. She had had to leave everything behind, but her sister and brother-in-law had got out of Germany much earlier and had been able to bring their furniture, so once inside their flat one felt no longer in England. They have the biggest chest I have ever seen, 14th century of reddish-coloured oak with figures in relief – Maximilian riding into Munich. Also there is an enormous 14th century carved, inlaid cabinet, a huge gloomy picture of Christ and two great bronze candlesticks. The atmosphere is altogether baronial and a fine setting for her large handsome figure. H and he talked music. He thinks Schubert the most amazing musical genius the world has produced. I was pleased at this for I love Schubert the most though I don't think I agree about his *supreme* genius. The Ulrich boy, aged twelve, has been reading Gibbon at my suggestion and seems to enjoy him. 'He flows along like a great river,' he said.

DECEMBER 16TH

To Farm with presents for Moore and Stockwell children. Mrs Moore and baby (a boy) looking charming.

1939

The Addy baby born next door and almost the same day is a poor little thing, Mrs M says she is sure it is because Mrs Addy smoked all the time she was pregnant. Collected holly, potatoes, vegetables and boots; the drive home was bitterly cold.

DECEMBER 17TH
To R. Club, prepared to read them 'Pickwick' but the musical game arranged by Mrs M. took up all the time. Mrs Israel spoke to me about getting her brother and son out of Germany. I will do what I can of course, but fear there is little hope.

DECEMBER 18TH
Shopped all the morning and afternoon for the Christmas tree party with Miss Heath who was a bit managing but I enjoyed getting presents for the little children especially a large bag of little ships and a delightful doll.

DECEMBER 21ST
Christmas Tree party. Lots of helpers, very cold. Tree looked thin and skinny, but better when dressed. It was a very happy party though not much room for games. The conjurer was good and very pleased with his audience – Carl, with his unexpected unselfconscious remarks, little Gunther with his polite bows and Ernst with his sense of humour. Parents delighted.

DECEMBER 23RD

All four drove to Tufton with Benny. The Farm and the country looking nice in cold, but sunny weather. H and I went to Winchester and the Cathedral service: the Cathedral so beautiful but the service depressing – the priest drawling it out as if nothing was more boring than the story of Christ's birth and the faces of the congregation looking grim. Everything seemed only half alive except the choir boys' voices, sounding detached and perfect, like the voices of stone cherubs. It was perishingly cold in the Cathedral.

CHRISTMAS DAY 1939

A quiet pleasant Christmas. Madeleine feeling better. At night, we took lamps and sang carols to Chris's flute playing outside the Farm cottages. It was a lovely frosty moonlit night and the carols were much appreciated except at the Powells' who had the wireless on so loudly they couldn't hear us.

DECEMBER 27TH

H drove off at midday in the Jowett. Jane I went for a walk in the late afternoon. I love these low rounded Hampshire hills; the sun was immense, a brilliant hard orange. We watched it *rushing* towards the earth, most peculiar it looked too. Ellen would have said it was a portent. Am reluctant to leave tomorrow and the children stay on here.

DECEMBER 28TH

Arrived with Ben at Whitchurch to hear the London train was already 45 minutes late at Salisbury. Jane and Bunny tried to persuade me to go back with them but decided against it though, after they had left, sitting in the bitterly cold waiting room with an utterly miserable little dog, I rather regretted it. The train was an hour late at Waterloo and outside the station a murky darkness had descended with extreme rapidity, Waterloo itself was like an unutterably gloomy underworld. A dreadfully long journey to Sevenoaks in dark unheated carriage full of dim shapes; Ben kept me from completely freezing. At Sevenoaks no taxis and I gave two shillings to a porter instead of one, but he brought me back the extra shilling! All the time the electric trains were flashing brilliantly without, though perfectly dark within. Home at last and H came in at 7.30. He too had had hateful journeys. Very glad to be home for him.

DECEMBER 30TH

Decided on Benenden for the weekend in spite of weather and found roads not too bad. After lunch walked to the village and then to Benenden Place where our late Irish cook, Annie, is in service, having distinctly bettered herself. We went round to the tradesmen's entrance and were greeted with enthusiasm by Annie. H went for a walk while I was regaled with china tea and a piece of Annie's marvellous Christmas cake and listened to all the gossip about 'the mistress' who came to the door while I was there, but didn't see me. One shilling's worth of cream to make ice cream for 25 people was what got

Annie. 'As for her husband she's brass on his buttons.'
Presently the Lady's maid came in and was introduced.
When H came back from his walk he, too, was given
tea. Annie talked of the I.R.A. – pretty serious she
thinks – 'Getting hold of all the young men. You never
know who you may be talking to. I found out they were
all around me one day so I got straight on my bicycle
and came back home and told my mother, but, glory
be, my brother Pat's having none of them. So I came
away to England as quick as may be. I didn't want to
be mixed up in anything of that kind. I had enough of
that as a child.'

DECEMBER 31ST

To Cranbrook to visit Violet [*the daughter of our much
loved 'char' of Blackheath days*] who has evacuated herself
and family to tiny Ivy Cottage there. Her husband is at
sea. Found her in much characteristic confusion, warmth
and cheerfulness. A joint was cooking in the oven and
the copper was heating for the weekly bath for her three
and one extra evacuee child. Violet's children are like
marigolds with bright golden hair and round open faces:
the room overflowing with toys, clothes and cardboard
boxes. Violet, quite unconcerned at the chaos, took us
over the cottage. She has all her mother's good temper
and generosity but is not so intelligent or capable. Back
to Sevenoaks in the evening. What will 1940 bring? One
must just live a day at a time.

1940

JANUARY 3RD

To Oxford to visit Judith. A long, very cold drive and
Richard had eaten all the lunch by the time we got there!
The baby is charming and Judith an excellent mother.
What an entity mother and baby are compared to the
father, though Richard is more aloof than most. I slept
with the baby who is very good. The next day I went to
call on Spenny [*Janet Spens – English don at Lady Margaret Hall.*] who was very welcoming but tired. She nobly
has five evacuee children and only a daily woman: she
likes them though and they *love* her. She is a little sad
and worried about her memory and power of concentration going.

JANUARY 6TH

Home again. This afternoon the children had Alison A
and Margaret H to tea, both of whom we have known
for a dozen or more years. I thought at tea how nice
the four of them were, sincere, cheerful, sensible and
affectionate creatures – poor dears, I do hope life will
give them something better in the future than it offers

them now. H has gone next door to play violin sonatas with Jestyn Jones. After tea I retired to the sitting room with Priestley's *Rain upon Gadshill*. Bursts of laughter came up from below and sounds of Mozart and Schubert through the wall. I was happy alone and yet not at all lonely. Priestley made me long to travel and see Arizona, and I like his mind, his mixture of romanticism and commonsense in just the right degree; he is very English.

JANUARY 8TH — 18TH

Chris and I having flu. This evening I played about with the wireless; there was nothing I especially wanted to hear, but sometimes the magic of it gets me. To lie in bed and idly twiddle knobs and to conjure into the silence of my bedroom a whole panting Variety Company, a huge orchestra from the heart of an 'enemy' country, an earnest French politician or a group of wild musicians wailing to a tom tom. What ancient princely potentate ever dreamed of so much power with so little effort.

E has come to help us and is so kind, cheerful and tireless, but very hopeless at any household affairs. H, too, has had suppressed flu and because of this and the awful weather and war conditions of travelling, has not been home much. I hate seeing so little of him, our lives seem to have got too separate by night and day.

FEBRUARY 8TH — 11TH

News bad from Finland. [*Russia attacked Finland in 1939. In early 1940 France and England were preparing an Expeditionary force to help the Finns but Finland capitulated in 1940.*] At Benenden alone to try and recover from post-flu tiredness and giddiness: a queer time of peace and loneliness; the loneliness was only oppressive in the evenings and because the weather was dismal, the snowdrops only just showing; the rabbits and pigeons have eaten all the sprout tops; the geese are making very little noise, subdued by the cold I think. Reading Cobbett's *Advice to a Youth*, which is charming in its wise simplicity and the tenderness he shows towards his family and very amusing in its self-confidence and cocksuredness. Also finishing Fielding's *Jonathan Wilde*, a perfect piece of satirical writing, neither bitter nor sentimental. He is very pacifist.

FEBRUARY 27TH

Thaw at last, but after the partial thaw there was another cold night and a most beautiful white frost and long icicles, everything intricate and shining. To London to hear Madriaga [*the Spanish diplomat*]. He was good and very lucid. He said we were fighting not because Germany was wicked but because our Empire was threatened!

MARCH 28TH

To the Refugee Club. Evening began with some rather badly played Elizabethan music for which I had to propose a vote of thanks. Then followed the refugees' own play, a very spirited performance. It started with an office in Berlin selling permits to England for enormous sums. Next came a scene at the English Embassy with a secretary trying to cope with a queue of women, none of whom had done any housework before, and all of whom were ready to do anything from a governess to a kitchen maid. They were all sent to Sevenoaks! The last scene was at the Club with a tiny oil stove in the background and the refugees being welcomed with 'good afternoon, we are so sorry we can't get any coal again but we have a splendid programme or 15th century music and a lecture on English prepositions!' It is marvellous that they can make fun of their misfortunes and us in this way and they acted with such verve and abandon.

APRIL 9TH

Very bad news: Germany has invaded Denmark and Norway. Went with Jane to see Galsworthy's 'Skin Game' done at the Tonbridge Rep. Well done but too miserable about the news to enjoy it.

APRIL 10TH

To Second Wednesday Lunch Club and felt encouraged a little by Sir Frederick White's very interesting talk on America and also by Mrs Seligman, looking like a Gainsborough portrait in green, with violets, and so calm and lovely still.

APRIL 11TH

To Benenden to find Stockwell there on leave and very excited about a naval victory at Narvik. I felt temporarily better because of this and the beauty of the country, but very anxious about Scandinavia and especially worried about Mary Knudsen and family in Denmark, and Eva in Bergen, and am so sick of bloodshed, horror and hate.

APRIL 12TH

Lovely walk to the marshes where Ben went quite wild with joy. Back to Sevenoaks regretfully in the evening with vegetables and wild daffodils picked in the meadow behind the farm. I took the chair at night when Mr L spoke well on the War Registers International. But oh dear, how pacifists seem only to see one side of things and to simplify too much.

APRIL 13TH

My help, Peggy, hasn't turned up for two days. I had a committee meeting at 11 and Judith, Ruth, the refugee help, and baby came at 12.30. Baby is now very like Judith. It is so nice to have a baby in the family again. Peggy's sister Joan came to help as Peggy is ill and she would not take any money for it. Went to club to read poetry aloud for Dr Flucher who was lecturing on Shakespeare in German.

APRIL 19TH

Judith and Ruth to cinema so H and I had a quiet evening at home. He is very tired I fear, but so good. Finished Leonard Woolf's *Barbarians at the Gate*, good and clarifying.

APRIL 23RD

Helping get the International Exhibition ready and made a short speech at the opening – attendance not bad. I'm afraid poor Mrs L's beautifully executed, but quite undistinguished embroidery won't sell; her tragic face haunts me. To King Lear at the Old Vic with J, theatre packed. Gielgud made a speech saying what marvellous audiences they had had, though everyone had told him Lear would fail in war time. Fay Compton and Lewis Casson very good as Regan and Kent.

APRIL 25TH

My forty-second birthday. Nice picnic with the children and the Bickwells on the hills behind Shoreham. To the Refugee exhibition in the evening – takings not bad but *no* expensive exhibits sold. Four orders for the Heu plaques.

APRIL 28TH

Met a most interesting political refugee. He is 38 years old and was a journalist and a leader in the German Socialist Party. He was tortured in a concentration camp to make him betray his fellow socialists and escaped death miraculously through a mistake. He was let out instead of another prisoner of the same name and fled to Czechoslovakia and then to England. He has red hair and a strong, well modelled face. He is neither depressed nor bitter and thinks the economic collapse of Germany fairly sure in about three years time, and then that a democratic government will be possible. I tried to explain the pacifist point of view to him and said I felt very doubtful whether evil could ever be cast out by evil. He said, so gently: 'Well you see I hate Hitler and Nazism so much that I may not see clearly because hate is not good for vision.'

APRIL 29TH – MAY 3RD
To Whimple (Devon) to visit the parents. [*They had had to leave Hodcombe, their home on the Sussex Downs, and had evacuated themselves to a small guest house in this Devonshire village.*] The house is pleasant but undistinguished. The views and situation beautiful, woods and fields all round. They have a good sitting room to themselves and seem happily settled in. Mother busy with her Braille work and Dad with all sort of projects.

APRIL 30TH
Mother's 77th birthday; wet and cold. We went to Exeter to the cathedral. Dad very bossy. I wish I didn't get so irritated with him, it is childish and stupid but I can't seem to help it. He won't even let one look at the view in one's own way! 'Don't let your attention wander from those trees'! etc. I suppose it's a leftover from childhood,

but I'm always at my worst with him, argumentative and unsympathetic. I was glad really to get away, though Mother, as always, was so sweet.

MAY 9TH
Bad news from Norway.

MAY 10TH
Hitler invaded Holland and Belgium.

MAY 14TH
Holland gives in.

MAY 20TH — 27TH
Germany has succeeded in making a 25 mile break through the French line and has reached the coast at Boulogne. The French command has changed and our government entirely reorganized under Churchill. This fortnight has been too much of a nightmare to put down on paper. It is evident that the German military command is brilliant as well as ruthless and that both we and the French lack good leadership. Also we seem to be riddled with fifth column men: the collapse of Holland was mainly due to that. At any time now England may be invaded by air and subject to merciless bombing. Meanwhile normal life here goes on and this exquisite May is drawing to a close. Never has the country looked more lovely; the children are working hard for their

exams and we are trying to decide whether to buy pro-
perty to retire to and where. The position of America is
still obscure. Freda, my help, said: 'I hope to God they
come in, what we want is a few of their gangsters over
here to help us.'

H was to have gone to France on a scientific advisory
mission, but I am thankful to say it was cancelled at the
last moment. I am trying to make up my mind where, if
anywhere, I should send the children. Meanwhile friends
very comforting and we all support each other.

MAY 26TH
Day of national prayer – churches crowded.

MAY 27TH
In the evening caught the bus to Crouch to spend a night
with Ellen: noise of guns bad but not so clear as at
Benenden. We listened to the midnight news.

MAY 28TH
News terrible. King Leopold has capitulated and our
army is therefore cut off from the main body of the
French and cannot escape except by the coast. Ellen and
I thought we should be beaten. The house and garden
painfully lovely. Home after lunch and feel distinctly
better at home: French very bitter about King Leopold;
the Belgian Government have repudiated him. I am
trying all the time to decide about the children, should
they be sent away and if so where? Dorothy [*my sister*]

and family have all gone to Devonshire to Ashwater where Jess and Lawrence [*cousins*] are. Lawrence is now Vicar there. Our army fighting a desperate rear guard action to reach the coast.

MAY 30TH

Met Nancy Bicknell at Halstead. We lay in a lovely buttercup meadow between Twitton and Shoreham and talked war. We are both feeling less defeatist. I know now I couldn't bear us to give in. To club in the evening. Poor Rosa Schott, very depressed at losing her job here and now wants to go to London.

MAY 31ST

In the middle of supper a phone call came for me to say that Madeleine had had a son this evening. The baby wasn't expected till mid-July so she must have got her dates wrong as he isn't really very premature. M is pretty well. I am most relieved. After supper Jane read her very good paper on Pope to our little literature group. I felt we had had another happy evening wrested from old Hitler anyway. News better than we had hoped about the evacuation of our army.

JUNE 1ST

Disturbed night owing to arrival of the Jones baby next door. It began about 3 a.m. punctuated by heavy gun thuds. The boy arrived about 10.30 a.m. Jane and I heard the tiny cry. All this day troops on their way back from France coming through the town in charabancs and lorries past our house. Watched them through the window, the street lined with cheering people. They looked very tired but were singing loudly. It is a miracle that they are here. We drank the health of young Bomford and young Jones in ginger beer at lunch which Chris went and bought at old Budgeons'. Lord Gort has arrived in England. There are incredible stories of courage and daring, especially of the small craft; one boy of 15 went to and fro with his father in a motor boat completely unarmed to fetch off troops with bombs bursting all round: the navy busy washing and ironing the clothes of nurses they had picked up half drowned. Dunkirk has been strongly fortified by the French and Calais is still holding out. The news from Italy is bad.

I have agreed to take a class of 12 small girls in our sitting room from West Heath School (which is disbanded); to teach them history and English, but it probably won't materialize. At the end of this week I feel differently about the war. I do not think now that either the French or ourselves will ever give in; there may be treachery, we may be faced with invasion, Italy will probably come in on the Nazi side and America may not come to our aid, but we shall keep on through all and therefore will not lose in the end. But at what cost! However one gains fresh courage from the courage of others, and since the evacuation from Dunkirk I feel that for the first time Hitler has not had it all his own way.

JUNE 3RD

Wonderful weather this summer *so* almost mockingly beautiful. Walked with Jane to Shoreham, the old valley looking at its best and had tea in the garden with Mrs Baker at her cottage 'The Meadows'. She doesn't give teas any more but she gave us one. [*This cottage was completely destroyed later by a flying bomb.*]

JUNE 4TH

Raid on Paris injuring over 200 people. Attack on France begun again. Churchill's speech full of defiance and informed hope put new courage into me. I never appreciated the power of true oratory before.

JUNE 6TH

Perfect weather – letter from Madeleine about the baby which made a lump come in my throat: 'He is grand! He is very wee and he hasn't got his eyes open yet, but nurse says he hasn't got jaundice too badly.'

JUNE 8TH

Saw the baby next door Thomas Jestyn, who is very like his father. Went to swim with H at Dunton Green open air swimming baths. Very hot, gloomy over news, French being driven back.

1940

JUNE 18TH

In the evening listened to Churchill's broadcast and after it I again felt a real inrush of courage. He has the power to coin unforgettable phrases that light up something inside one.

JUNE 20TH – 24TH

These are probably the last days of our lovely, happy home life. On Monday came the news of the French capitulation. I was in London trying to get an exit permit for Chris to go to Canada where he has been offered a home by a Canadian Professor of Metallurgy, someone we don't know at all. We are touched and grateful. In the evening H was away and I felt too miserable to stay alone (the children were out) so I went next door and was slightly comforted by the smell and sounds of the baby. When H came home he told me that Judith was considering going to Canada with Rachel. The University of Toronto have invited all the children of Oxford University for the duration and the mothers with small babies. On Wednesday I went to Oxford to see Judith and say goodbye. Rachel is very handsome and jolly. Judith and I broke down at parting. Walked about Oxford (for the last time?). E came to lunch and is fairly cheerful, but she always is. All the week we have been trying to get the exit permit for Chris. If only he could go with Judith. Jane is very anxious not to go to Devon. I feel that to cling to the illusion that we can go on as we are is stupid and selfish, yet I try to keep things as normal as possible. On Friday Jane and I drove to Benenden. Approaching Goudhurst the police stopped us as it was the 20 mile limit from the coast and I had to establish my identity by phoning from the police station to Benenden village shop. Then the car refused to start again and we had three policemen and one postman pushing it for us – but in vain! Finally we had to walk up the hill and send a man from the garage down to it while we had an unsatisfactory lunch at Goudhurst. At last we got to the Farm, looking so peaceful and sunny with roses and honeysuckle in full bloom. We worked hard at collecting eggs, picking fruit etc. and got the car started again with the help of Addy and all three Wheelers [*farm hands*]. On Saturday news very bad: France almost certain to sign an armistice with terms directed primarily against us. It must only be a matter of days now before we get the full brunt of it. There have been air raids all this week, but not near enough for us to get a warning yet. Hal came to tea and after we all went to see Gracie Fields in a film called 'Sing as we go' – very good. This double life goes on; one's normal life on one plane of existence and on the other – complete uncertainty and parting and horror and the end of all security. I get attacks of intense homesickness for normality. Last week all our refugees had to leave Kent and we had a sad parting from them. I got the Glasses and the Immerglucks temporary homes elsewhere.

JUNE 24TH

First real air raid warning here went at about 1 a.m. Got down to the basement and I read Sylvia Townsend Warner's *Mr Fortune's Maggot* aloud. Family very cheerful but sleepy. Jane said: 'Ben must think we are quite mad.' H said: 'Well we are, aren't we?' After about half an hour as all seemed quiet I went back to bed and the others followed very soon. The All Clear went at 3.30. Some people only woke then and mistook it for a warning and stayed up all the rest of the night waiting for the All Clear.

JUNE 25TH

I suppose I was more tired than I knew for, by the evening, when my gooseberry jam set too stiffly, I felt completely wretched and couldn't help crying. Then Hal rang up to say that it was practically impossible to get Chris an exit permit. One just mustn't allow oneself to think what will happen to boys of his age if the Nazis get over here. Exit permits are not being issued now to boys over fourteen in case they should be needed for the forces later on I suppose. Chris is both relieved and disappointed.

JUNE 26TH

To London to meet E. Harvey at Friends House. Nice to see her again but she was tired and gloomy. She said bombs had been dropped in Dorset where her children are and this finally decided me not to send Jane to Devon against her will. Met her and we went to the Temple Church to hear Adele Fachere and Jelly d'Aranye. They played divinely – Bach, Handel, Mozart and Purcell. Jelly looked lovely in black with a flat, black, velvet cap – completely Renaissance. I felt much better for the music. I met C. Anson outside who had come from

Oxford. She said Dora was going to Canada with her two boys. The future looks immensely black, but I have recovered from the shock of French capitulation and keep cheerful making jam, gardening and doing odd jobs.

JUNE 29TH

To Benenden with H for the day, not much trouble with the police at Goudhurst this time. Very happy picking fruit, getting our simple meals, talking to people in the village. We all encourage each other. It was hard to leave and I *long* to be living here in peace. Lovely sky and scents coming home. Air raids every night but not much damage. What though is to come?

JULY 1ST

Very hot. Jane and I drove to Penshurst. The Polo ground on the way has been turned into a military camp and the hedges have all vanished. At Penshurst many troops passing through and the beautiful meadow below Penshurst gardens cut up with dug-outs, army lorries etc. But everything else lovely, Penshurst Place shone a pale green in the brilliant summer sun. We sat in a field with some glorious Jersey cows and then had a glass of cider at the little Angler's Arms. I ached for love of the English countryside and with hatred of all governments. In the evening made blackcurrant jam from the fruit we had brought back from the Farm and talked to Mrs A who has got her daughter to America, though she is over sixteen. Maddened by letters in the Times.

JULY 3RD

Anthea came for her birthday. I hadn't seen her since her sudden and private marriage to Gordon Roxbrough. She is unchanged as far as I can judge – very young, very pretty, very absorbed in her dog and cat. They hope to move to the Isle of Wight on Monday. German planes over us at tea time while we were absorbing the chocolate birthday cake.

JULY 8TH

Ellen came for the day as I am not allowed now to go to Crouch as it is a restricted area. She was the usual mixture of wisdom and foolishness. Air raids continue every day and night, but no harm here yet. They have had raids even in Devon and Cornwall which makes me very glad we didn't send Jane away.

JULY 16TH

Jitters about imminent German invasion. Chris at school, making Molotov cocktails, i.e. home made bombs to throw at invaders as they come through Sevenoaks. He told me what they were made of in detail – it is horrible to think of schoolboys thus employed and I can't think it will be of the slightest use.

   To London to shop. Met H for National Gallery concert – (a lovely Haydn quartet) and felt cheered by the music. Afterwards went to exhibition of war pictures. Artizzoni (who seems to me to be a mixture of Daumier and Rowlandson), Anthony Gross (very clever pen and

ink sketches), Ravilion (good colour and design) and fine
heads by Eric Kennington.

JULY 20TH

Cable to say that Judith and baby have arrived safely.
Heard that a bomb had dropped at Brighton in Aunty
Ada's back garden, blowing part of the wall away. She
is alright, but suffering from shock.

JULY 29TH

H took the day off and we went to Benenden. Henley
(the farmer) has at last consented to sell us the Farm
House with the field opposite and the little wood. We
went first to the house agent, a fat, talkative, nice man
who lost a leg in the 1914 war and has had pain every
day since. We then went to the Farm and dug two rows
of potatoes to take back with carrots and apples. Then
we went for a walk in *our* wood. In the wood we met
our dear white cat, Perkin, purring and welcoming like
a guardian spirit. He walked back with us. He is now
nine years old and the best and cleverest cat in the world,
and has never caught a bird. The wood has oak, ash,
willow and hazel and a lovely little gulley with ferns. We
shall clear the undergrowth and do some planting. The
day began with rain and greyness and I thought would
not be a success but, as ever here it *was* and we were
very happy not thinking or talking about the war. Jane
away, taking her exams at Letchworth. I miss her greatly
but am so thankful the Blitzkrieg hasn't started yet,
though I can't be so optimistic as E or Miss B, who both

think that Hitler is not able to attack. America's views about coming into the war more hopeful and Roosevelt has been nominated unanimously for a third term. Hitler now says he is going to attack us at the beginning of August. I have written to resign from the P.P.U. I am miserable about this but I find I can't be a wholehearted pacifist in this war against Nazism. Have read lately with great pleasure, Adrian Seligman's account of his Voyage in the Cap Pillar; with pleasure, Ethel Smythe's *As Time goes on*; with amusement Robert Graves' *Antigua Penny Price* and with boredom Pritchett's *Nothing like Leather*.

JULY 28TH

The immediate strain of waiting for the Blitzkrieg has eased a little, but one would like to know what Hitler is waiting for. There are small raids every day in which we bring down more planes than we lose, and raids by us on military objectives which are said to be successful. That's all at present. The terrible 'Aliens' business affecting the poor refugees, not to speak of *all* foreigners in Britain, is at last being raised owing to public agitation and the Press, but Sir John Anderson wants watching. [*Sir John Anderson, then Home Secretary, was responsible for policy regarding the refugees from Germany in Great Britain and it was this that I felt wanted watching. I was all too right.*]

It has rained every day since St Swithins!

AUGUST 4TH

At Benenden. We must let the Farm, alas, until we are able to live there and the house agents have found us tenants, so we have hurried down to meet them. They seem ideal, a young couple called Cooper, both very handsome! He owns 200 acres of land in Walkhurst Lane and has a brother living there. But they want it for three years and at once! I can't bear the idea of not coming here for three long years; it has been my boon and comfort for the past three, but it is no use feeling sad about it and we've got it to come to in the end, unless the war destroys it. We drove to Tenterden after seeing these people. The raid warning went while we were shopping, but no one took the slightest notice. We asked a shopkeeper, smoking a pipe in a doorway, if there was a public shelter. He said no and that if the planes were overhead it didn't mean anything – you could be sure you were all right as they would have dropped their bombs already.

AUGUST 5TH

Breakfast out of doors. Talked to the charcoal burners, who are here – camped out beyond the pond. It is a skilled job and both men had been doing it all their lives. The elder was now seventy-four. He said few have the patience to go in for it now, though charcoal is badly needed. The younger man does forestry in the winter. The wood is arranged in beautifully neat, round piles and the spaces filled with dried bracken etc., then it is fired and left burning for four days. It must never go out. It was a perfect evening again, crowds of swallows and martins swooping round and skimming the pond. When it got dark we could see the glow from the charcoal piles and the dim shapes of the quiet charcoal burners against the night sky.

AUGUST 14TH

Barbara's son Roger born. Saw Jane off to Tufton Warren where Chris now is, helping with the harvest. Then met E and went with her to the Academy Cinema to see 'La Femme du Boulanger', a wonderful French film. Coming home at Knockholt the guard came to tell us that there was a raid on and the train slowed down, but did not stop and everyone began talking to each other. We saw smoke in different directions and at Sevenoaks were warned to get into an air raid shelter, which we did for a short time and then started to walk home before the All Clear. This was the first raid on Croydon and all the enemy planes were destroyed.

AUGUST 15TH

To lunch with Ellen at Crouch. First, in order to be allowed to enter the defence area, I had to get an order to view a bungalow for sale in the village! Then, just as I was starting the sirens went. I sat in the garage till the All Clear. I went from Ightham by the back lanes in order to avoid being stopped by the police and got lost. I stopped at a cottage to ask the way and thought the people looked a bit surprised and, going on, gradually became aware of the noise of planes and guns. This got louder and nearer and I was very relieved when I suddenly recognized where I was. I left the car and ran into Crouch Farm House. Ellen met me horrified, as by now the combat overhead was pretty close. We sat in the inglenook till things were fairly quiet. When I set off for home the warning went again but it didn't seem too bad so I went on. H was late owing to raids.

AUGUST 16TH

At Benenden for weekend. A long raid of about 2 hours. The planes were very high – too high to see but there were curious lines of white smoke in the sky with waves of black crossing them. We heard that there were about 600 German planes over – several brought down near Tenterden. At High Halden they came low and machine gunned people, including Addy and little Tom. Felt very tired when it was over – another short raid later.

The workmen came on Monday and began to move out our things. The Coopers came over, very beautiful and quite nice. Got off at about five o'clock, tired and rather melancholy.

AUGUST 19TH

To Tufton with Ben. Everyone was jaded after the visit of a German plane which dropped a bomb in the field. Chris came in after tea looking sunburnt but tired. He had thought the house hit last night. He seemed very pleased I had come.

AUGUST 20TH

Everyone more cheerful after a good night. Benny is settling down in the eggery. Robert is a very good looking and pleasing baby. Country lovely. H arrived safely. German plane over and machine gun fire but no bombs. Harvest is nearly over and very good, one glorious field of flax still in bloom.

AUGUST 26TH

Home with H, stopping on the way to shop and go to the National Gallery concert (Handel). Raid while in the train, lady in carriage who lived at Cranbrook, said they had had bombing there, do hope they don't get the Windmill or the Church. Madeleine has sent me home with chicken and eggs as usual. She is so generous.

AUGUST 29TH

To Cheltenham, [*where my two sisters-in-law lived together*] Georgiana ill and pathetic. Every night at about 10 pm air raids begin. Elizabeth never hears the explosions and always talks on and on through them. Even a screaming bomb quite near she only thought was Georgiana calling out. I hated the evening, worst when H was expected at 10. He was an hour late with a raid going on all the time. Lovely relief when he came and having him through the night. Spent the days reading aloud Trollope to Georgiana and listening to Elizabeth. Whether because of escape from the house or as a contrast to the raided nights, I deeply enjoyed one evening's walk. The town and its surrounding hills shone with a

strange beauty and I was possessed of them as Traherne
was when he wrote:

'The streets were paved with golden stones. . .
In joy and beauty they appeared to me.
And everything which here I found,
While like an Angel I did see
Adorned the ground.'

AUGUST 30TH

Sad parting with Georgiana; I fear it may be for the last
time. I do long for her to have another existence more
fulfilled and happier than this life has offered her.

AUGUST 31ST TO SEPTEMBER 3RD

A different world here at Northcourt House. No raids
and, on the whole, a very cheerful family. Mrs Tatham
has a sweet silly nurse who never stops talking: 'My last
patient had five hundred budgies, too many I call it, well
don't you? Five hundred budgies!' 'I'm very fond of
little children; it's naughty of me but that's how I am.'
'The world's very small I think' – etc. etc. Evelyn and
I had one perfect day from another world sketching at
Lechlade. We met two lovely elephants on the way! Sat
in the churchyard, swallows and swifts in a cloud round
the spire. Some children came by and admired and com-
mented; later, when I was crouching down in the shadow
of a grave stone to avoid the sun on my block, I heard
what I took to be another child stop behind me. 'Now
run along,' I said crossly without looking up, 'as if it

wasn't bad enough having no shade, I can't have you bothering round.' Silence, I then did look and it was the Vicar! He was quite nice but not amused. We had bread and cheese at an old Inn, then lay in the sun and then decided to bathe in the river. We had to undress in the ladies cloakroom; I was so hot I felt sick, but the bathe was utterly delicious. Afterwards we walked across the meadows to the Trout Inn where there was a huge walnut tree and flowers against the Cotswold wall. Back to Northcourt House and a golden evening. Roast duck for supper. This has been a day recreated from a pre-war existence.

While in Oxford I have decided on Jane going there to go to the Slade which is evacuated there. Perhaps she could live with the Frys. I am not without qualms but must decide something.

SEPTEMBER 4TH – 12TH

A horrid week alone each day. H late every night. Getting used to raids. Churchill thinks invasion imminent. His speeches are pretty marvellous; never minimizing danger or bad news, but always full of courage and hope and such splendid oratory.

SEPTEMBER 12TH

Set off cheerfully to meet Jane at Redhill. She is coming back from Tufton; Chris is staying on to work on the farm, I had spent the previous night on the dining room floor, the Jones family in the basement. A peaceful drive to Redhill station where I saw a notice 'Paterson's Taxis'

and remembered my childhood and Mr Paterson in his
top hat and his wife with her gruff voice and untidy hair
and waiting in a little hut beside a bright fire for one of
Mr Paterson's 'growlers' to take us home. Of course they
have both long been dead. I had a cup of coffee at
Cooke's Restaurant which is still recognizable, though
the beautiful bead curtains have gone. I used to admire
them so much when I came here with my mother on the
top of a horse-bus as a great treat to have a glass of milk
and a bun and to chat to Mrs Cooke who had little twin
girls. I was comforted by these memories which belonged
to another world than this – a sane world, and I told
myself firmly it was as real as the present nightmare. I
then went to Redhill station where I waited for 1½ hours
for the train to come in. I was surrounded by soldiers
and by crowds of refugees from London, from Ashford,
from Canterbury – many tired and frail and bewildered
and with no settled destination. It was cold and I was
worried as to whether I should miss Jane in the crowd
or perhaps she had got out at Dorking and was waiting
for me there. At last, however the train arrived and she
was on it and at once everything became cheerful. We
had a good hot meal at Cooke's Restaurant and a good
talkative journey home. At night H, Jane and I all slept
in the basement with the Joneses and it was much quieter
there.

SUNDAY SEPTEMBER 15TH
H and I went for a walk and the warning went when we
were in the woods beyond Oak Lane. On the way home
fighting became louder and nearer and planes were dart-

ing about in great numbers. Just by the Church a group of fighting planes got very low and near, and the rattle of machine gun fire became terrific. We began to run for it. Wardens shouted out, 'Take cover!' but all doors were shut. We reached home panting and weak about the knees. I picked up a bullet on our doorstep. Heard afterwards that there had been a big air battle today.

SEPTEMBER 16TH

Children's Exam results came through – both have done very well. Went with Jane to Ellen's at Crouch. She was very cheerful. We had tea with an exquisite little artist called Denton Welch. He lives in an odd modern house at Platt with marvellous 18thC and Chinese furniture and china and he gave us tea in beautiful cups without handles. He lives alone with a sinister housekeeper looking like Beatrix Lehmann. Denton showed us all his things with childlike pleasure and enthusiasm. A bomb had made a hole in his garden but none of his precious things had suffered. Raid just after tea and, as usual I felt more unsafe in other people's homes.

Two family poems:

To our German Raider by Jane
Here Cuthbert comes whom Fate allots
A second Santa Claus
To visit Kentish chimney pots
With unexpected stores
He plies his way, serene, alert
To soothe our wakeful Borough
Still muttering: 'You can't beat Bert

Slow, slow, my boys but thorough.
Yet spite this obvious industry
In common duty's plight
We cannot miss him in the sky
Nor greet him as we might;
But whisper wide from far and near,
As Cuthbert wings above
A plane whom there are crowds to hear,
Yet very few to love.

To the Sevenoaks Sirens by H
Blest pair of syrens – like as any peas
Whom gloomy souls unkindly call Banshees
Renew your howls, always so 'grim and gay'.
And steel our hearts again from night to day

SEPTEMBER 22ND
Walthamstow Hall School was bombed last night. Thank God there were only 37 boarders there and miraculously no one was hurt other than a few cuts from broken glass. The new laboratory and craft rooms and the gym were destroyed and damage throughout all the buildings. The children have been billeted out in the town and teaching is going on in small groups. Everyone is undaunted and Miss Ramsay (the headmistress) was heard to say, when a cheerful crowd gathered among the ruin. 'I only wish Hitler could see us now.'

1940

All at Oxford. H went on to Cheltenham. I had a busy time, seeing Prof. Schwabe at the Slade and Letty Stack [*headmistress of Oxford High School*] about English coachings for Jane. It is all fixed up satisfactorily. She is to start at the Slade and also work for L.M.H. entrance and she and Christle Bergson are to live in Richard's flat. [*Christle and her parents were refugees from Vienna who came to Sevenoaks.*] Christle has to get government permission but we don't expect any difficulty. She is studying history of art and is charming. These 3 nights at Oxford have been a wonderful rest from raids.

OCTOBER 1ST – 12TH

Except for bad raids a pleasant time at home with both the children. A lunch with Denton Welch at Tunbridge Wells. News of London and of the mess over Dakar very depressing.

Drove Jane to begin her term at Oxford. The car broke down at Newlands Corner and had to be pushed by both of us.

OCTOBER 14TH

Jane started at the Slade. I went to call on Spenny who was fairly cheerful except about going senile. Noting her Warden's helmet in the hall, I said I hoped she did not have to go and stand about whenever there was a raid. She said, 'No dearie, I can see my beat from my window.' The idea of Spenny of all people having a beat – the most impractical and vaguest of the dons.

OCTOBER 16TH

Woke up feeling wretched with cold etc. and realized I could not drive home that day. Bad raids in London last night and muddle and difficulty about phoning H. The Mackintoshes, where I was staying, were very kind. Jane came round to tea and brought me the last chocolate peppermint creams left in Oxford! There was a warning in the evening – very unusual here and I did not move from my room, but there was great excitement in the household – old Bogey calling out for her money and refusing to go downstairs without it.

OCTOBER 19TH

Drove home, a damp, murky, cold day and car broke down at Benson – misery! Walked to garage and after an hour at last got away. News came through from Cheltenham that Georgiana had died. Bad raid and very noisy nights.

The day after I got home H went to Cheltenham for the funeral. It took him ten hours to get there – from 10 am to 8 pm. From the roof of our house there is a good view of the barrage balloons, like great silver hippopotami floating in the sky. They are at the same time beautiful and comic and comforting. I wonder if they are any good.

OCTOBER 21ST

Very wet day and therefore quieter in the air. Up to the present apparently Sevenoaks and the district around came second to London in the number of bombs dropped. In the town itself Youngs' old shop and the cottages behind the Lime Tree Hotel and the Club Hall have all been destroyed. In London – John Lewis, Peter Robinson, St James, Piccadilly, the Inn's Temple Hall and part of Pump Court and Holland House and many other buildings.

OCTOBER 22ND

A glorious day. Called at the Chantry and then took Ben for a walk in Knole park to pick up chestnuts. An air battle going on above all the time, lines of white weaving themselves all over the high blue sky. The trees, deer and Knole all perfect in the unusually clear and brilliant light. Asked Jestyn Jones from next door to supper as Mary is away with the baby. I miss her but it simplifies sleeping arrangements in our basement. Finished as much of Sacheverell Sitwell as I wanted to read. Quiet night.

OCTOBER 23RD

To the Chantry to do up parcels of clothes for the homeless. Went to 'The Grapes of Wrath', an exceedingly good film, faithful to the book. Very moving. News about France and Spain disquieting. Hitler is trying to get France to declare war on us. A sinister meeting between Hitler, Ribbentrop, Laval and Franco. What will come of these meetings? Just as we seem to have got the better of the bombing.

OCTOBER 27TH

Constant raids all yesterday and throughout the night.
Bombs fairly near woke me at 4 o'clock. Walked to
Kippington Road to Hal's, who said there had been a
bomb on the BBC killing four people [*my brother in law
Hal Cummings was working at the BBC now as Foreign
Public Relations officer advising on foreign broadcasts*].
Went into the Jones' flat where Jestyn, Chris and H
played violin and piano Mozart Sonatas. Raid constant
at night and news about France disquieting.

OCTOBER 29TH

Lovely walk, picked spindleberries. The view across the
valley bright with autumn colours. In the ploughed fields
a group of people like peasants in a Breugel painting,
one with a bright red coat, another in a blue dress,
were leisurely following a horse and harrow picking up
potatoes; German planes overhead. John Barber came in
the evening to play trios with H and Chris, but poor H
got home too late.

OCTOBER 30TH

Greeks are holding out against Italy for the time being.
Hope Turkey will help. To Nancy Bicknell who was
gloomy about the war as usual, but otherwise cheerful.
A woman in the bus going home asked the bus driver
whether it was safe to go to Dartford by bus; 'Safe as
houses,' he said. 'Once you're on the bus and it's going
you won't know you're being bombed.' H came home
in the train in darkness with a woman and her baby and

dogs whose house had been bombed the night before. She was perfectly cheerful and uncomplaining, only enthusiastic about the shelter which had saved their lives.

OCTOBER 31ST

Walked to Otford in the morning. Saw two craters in fields towards Rye Lane where the electric cable had been hit last night. Met Charlie Browning who told me that Hodge [*our old gardener*] had been badly shaken by the bomb on Leonard Avenue. Then, walking up to the Ivens, who should I meet but Hodge himself. He looks much older and walks very lame and is very sad about his bombed home, but seemed most glad to see me and talk to me and enquired so anxiously about H. It touched me and made me feel I should have looked him up earlier. He said, 'I *should* like to get out of it for a time.' The loss of their homes to the old is especially terrible and pathetic. He is living with his son at present. Ralph Ivens looks *very* thin and tired. Nice evening with Chris and H; for a *wonder* the All Clear went at 9 pm so we went to bed in our own rooms though the warning went at 3.30 am and planes and bangs rather a nuisance for a time.

NOVEMBER 1ST

The Times is very hopeful about Greece holding out; we are already giving naval and air help. I very much want a job and don't know what to do about it.

Margaret G's brother has been killed; a paragraph in

the *Times* describes how he lost his life, deliberately guiding his machine so that it should not come down on houses, but which was obviously fatal to himself. I saw too in the *Times* that John Mather had been killed and a letter from Dick (his father) came by the next post. Poor Marie; it seems to make it worse that she is German and that her brother and Dick's brother fought on opposing sides in the 1914 war and were both killed. Bill Emmanuel also killed.

Committee meeting at Chantry at which I had to act as secretary. H away. Chris played in a school match and got a bad black eye. We went together to 'My son, my Son' by Howard Spring, not a bad film. Home in pitch darkness – no gleam of light anywhere. Not much sound of planes.

NOVEMBER 3RD
Pouring with rain all day. Enjoyed quiet time with Chris – chess in the evening. No warning at night because of weather I suppose. One at 5 am, but 10 hours without a warning is a record.

Miss Ramsay rang up this afternoon and there is a chance of my getting the job of English mistress at Walthamstow Hall next term. [*This school was started at Walthamstow in 1838 for the daughters of Non-conformist missionaries. In 1882 it moved to Sevenoaks and began to take day girls as well as boarders. These steadily increased and after the Butler Act it became a Direct Grant School though it still kept its distinct missionary boarding side. During the war the missionary children were an especial care as they were of course separated entirely from their parents for the duration. A number of the younger children were evacuated to Shropshire under the charge of members of the staff where they were visited regularly by Miss Ramsay.*]

NOVEMBER 5TH

Went to Crouch and enjoyed it, but tiresome journey back owing to time bombs all over Ightham. H home in the evening I am thankful to say. He does fire watching regularly at the Research Offices at Euston. Cheered by news of Roosevelt's re-election and also by Greek resistance.

NOVEMBER 7TH

Tea with Miss Ramsay to discuss teaching job. I think I shall get it if Miss C can't come back (she is nursing her mother). Do hope I make a success of it – terrified of course; rather depressed by fact that salary will be much reduced by income tax payable on H's and my *joint* income. Bombs every night but mostly before 10 pm and after 3 am. Went to have my blood transfused at St Nicholas Hall – the last time I was here was for a Pacifist Meeting. You lie on your back with a hot water bottle on your tummy and clasp a rubber bone in your hand. (Apparently my veins are deep and difficult to get hold of.) Afterwards you lie in a deck chair for 20 minutes and are given a cup of tea. I chatted to my fellow transfusers – a working class man who had been badly wounded in the last war, a farmer's daughter and a fashionable young Sevenoaks sprig.

NOVEMBER 12TH

A nice day – walked with Benny in Knole. In afternoon Chris played Chopin, Schubert and Mozart on the Jones' piano and then we went to see Micky Rooney in 'The Boyhood of Tom Edison'. M. Rooney good but film sentimental. Came out of the cinema into a perfect night though guns booming very loudly and German planes overhead.

NOVEMBER 12TH

To lunch with Elizabeth Buxton (an old L.M.H. friend living at Hildenborough, niece of Miss Jex Blake who had been Principal of L.M.H.). She was very much herself, imperturbable and efficient as usual. The butler made me nervous at lunch and Mrs Buxton looked so like J. B. that it put me out. The house is enormous. In the bus going home the woman bus conductor told me how she hated having to bicycle home at night through the air raids. I tried to comfort her by saying that with all the bombs dropped on Sevenoaks last Friday only one man was killed. She said, 'Yes but how do I know I shan't be the next one!'

NOVEMBER 20TH

Rachel Heath from the Chantry came in today. She has been in charge of seventy people in a Bermondsey shelter each night; all very well behaved; one man didn't come in one night because he suspected himself of being drunk; one little woman insisted on going to bed in her boots and toque. The shelter has now become uninhabitable owing to flooding and she is going back to her railway arches. The people are very disappointed because they are not going to be allowed to decorate the shelters for Christmas for fear of fire so Rachel said they would string sausages up instead! She is a wonderful person. I offered to go with her to the arches for a few nights from December 3rd if I were needed. I hope I shan't be though! Today 170 air raid victims were buried at Coventry. H at Wimbledon with the Seligmans for the night. I hate him being away.

NOVEMBER 24TH

When paying Budgeon's bill I mentioned that I had had a touch of gastric flu and he recommended cinnamon sticks boiled in a little water. This cure was told to old Mrs Budgeon by a nurse who had served under Florence Nightingale in the Crimean War! It worked.

NOVEMBER 25TH

To Walthamstow Hall. Interviewed by Miss Ramsay. She is plump, pale and unwieldy, but her face beams with intelligence and humour. She asked me about my pacifism: 'Does your husband approve?' I said, 'No, he doesn't approve of pacifism but he does approve of me.' I said I had had no experience of class teaching, only of coaching. She said would I read out a child's essay aloud to a class. I had no idea whether I would or no, but it seemed rather a framed question so I said 'No, not without the child's permission,' which was the right answer! I think she intends to have me. I went and listened to a few lessons – some impressively efficient and clear, some rather dull – especially a poetry class taken by Miss S who is filling in as English teacher for the time being.

NOVEMBER 27TH

Chris in bed with temperature – no other symptoms. Miss S to tea. I found her difficult to talk to. She was a bit patronizing and pedantic. She criticized the BBC for their use of the gerund and the school for their non-use of the colon. She seems to think punctuation the be-all and end-all. I am sure she is a clearer thinker and better informed than I am, but I hope I am right in believing I am more likely to interest the children. Chris still in bed with temperature and swollen glands. Very cold.

Heard with relief that the Bermondsey Settlement do not want me urgently for the shelter next week because I don't think Chris will be well enough to leave. Finished Howard Spring's *Fame is the Spur* – an interesting novel based on a study of Ramsay Macdonald. Two fairly near bombs have exploded just as I finished writing this entry. In Budgeon's shop this morning, tiny frail old Mrs B was surrounded by a crowd of Sevenoaks School boys – (the shop serves as a tuck shop for the day boys). All were so nice and polite: 'May I have two penny worth of gums please Mrs Budgeon?' 'Thank you very much Mrs Budgeon, goodbye Mrs Budgeon.' Read aloud to Chris *Those Days* by E. C. Bentley. He first wrote that lovely book *Biography for Beginners* in a note book with G. K. Chesterton when he was only sixteen. He invented *Trent's Last Case* while walking to and fro to Fleet Street.

NOVEMBER 30TH – DECEMBER 4TH

Time spent entirely in nursing Chris who has an obscure sort of flu. H away Sunday morning till Tuesday evening. Desperately worried and depressed about bad air raids on provincial towns and submarine warfare. Greek news continues to be the only cheering gleam [*Mussolini had attacked Greece and had been repulsed until Hitler sent German troops there in 1941.*] Learning Shakespeare's sonnets by heart. H is also doing this.

This morning had the following rather delightful letter from Mrs Heu (from Ampleforth where Berti and his brother are now at school):

'Dearest Mrs Moore,

We were delighted to hear from you again and it is very kind of you to remember Berti's birthday which is at the 26th. He adores Nesbit's books more than anything and is just very short of reading material. Thank you very much to care for him as usual. He always speaks from a model aeroplane which your Christopher sometimes gave him and which he forgot to take with him. He would be delighted to get it occasionally. He does very well at school, has excellent reports and is a highly esteemed goal keeper.

Ever yours,

Lille Heu.

DECEMBER 9TH

To Oxford with Chris where he is sitting for entrance to Merton. Bad London raid last night so we had to change at New Cross and then go in packed train to Whitechapel – from thence to Charing X and finally reached Padding-

ton. Crowds very cheerful and good tempered, one workman from the packed platform shouted out 'Germany
calling, Germany calling the British Isles' in Lord Haw
Haw's voice, making us all laugh. Chris very tired, but
cheered up at Oxford having tea with Jane. Then leaving
Chris at Merton to Northcourt, dear Northcourt, now
accommodating, besides the family, two evacuated
schoolmistresses and the artist Miss Brickdale. E is
working at the Food Office in Abingdon. News from
Egypt good. [*Again the Italians were doing badly against
the allies in Egypt* until *the Germans came to their help
under Rommel.*] Jane is getting on very well at the Slade,
but there is trouble with Richard about both the girls.
He is no doubt fractious and difficult but must be missing Judith badly. News from her good. Chris rather
gloomy.

DECEMBER 20TH

Went with H to stay the weekend with the Mathers at
Ifield. John's young widow was there; Marie talked to
me till late about John.

Chris rang us up at tea time to say he had won a very
good scholarship (postmastership they call it at Merton).
We are thrilled at this and it is most unexpected. He is
only just seventeen and was taking the exam as a 'trial
run'. Also he wasn't feeling a bit well at the time.

DECEMBER 22ND

Home. Hal came to tea rather tired and depressed owing
to his room having been bombed at the BBC and so he

has to work in the basement and he says everything is terribly crowded and difficult.

CHRISTMAS DAY 1940

A light fall of snow made everything looked very Christmasy. Good walk in Knole, cold but windless, no one about. We might have owned the park. Dear Matty had cooked our Christmas dinner and gave me her own copy of T. Moore's poems as a present. C. and J. had also made me wonderful presents. Listened to King's broadcast and to pathetic messages from evacuated children in Canada and U.S.A. to their parents. We had already heard from Judith. The Jones family came in for the evening and we had carols accompanied by C on the flute and H and Mary's sister on violins. No signs of war all day or night – a Christmas to remember, for us, with thankfulness, still united, still with a roof over our heads, but the thought of all those who have suffered so deeply makes one wonder about the paradox of thankfulness.

DECEMBER 27TH

Raids began again. Both the children are so charming to me and altogether lovable – seventeen is a lovely age and I can't help thinking they are both practically perfect – so there!

DECEMBER 30TH

Bad raids on London last night – the Guildhall burned and eight City churches – the best of Wren gone.

DECEMBER 31ST

Up to London with the children. Saw Chaplin in 'The Great Dictator'. There were two sublime bits – the dance with the world and when he shaves to Brahms' Hungarian Dance. The likeness to Hitler (a sort of Jekyll and Hyde) and the fact that they were both born on the same day is surely remarkable. The mixture of tragedy and broad farce I found upsetting at times. Shakespeare did it I know, but his was comedy rather than farce. The end is weak.

We came out of the cinema into the stricken streets, Leicester Square was full of blackened ruins. Jane said, 'What a world! And to think it is all true.' Rain was slowly falling and the air smelt of sour burning. We rushed into the National Gallery for coffee and sandwiches and went down into the basement shelter for the concert. It was cold but nice and it is easier to concentrate here than in the Dome. Lovely Mozart quartet. Out in time to get to see 'Berkeley Square' with Jean Forbes Robertson, decidedly older than when I last saw her, but voice unchanged and play, though not holding quite the same magic for me, still charming. A long, dark, cold journey home but a very successful Christmas treat day enjoyed fully by all. Sucks to Hitler!

1941

JANUARY 4TH

To Tufton in bitter wind and snow for the weekend. Madeleine seemed very glad to see me. Bunny in bed with a cold. Robert is a sweet and intelligent baby but much less forward in his movements than his twin, little Tom Jones. The evacuees, Daisy and Rosie, are a wonderful pair. After three minutes of meeting me Daisy began to tell me all about her husband. 'I've lost a good man, I have. Every evening I could have my bottle of stout or my cup of cocoa just as I wished.' She also gave me a history of Rosie's periods and showed me her new pink flannel petticoat. They seem very happy. 'Oh Rosie aren't you glad we've been bombed!'

M, with her usual kindness gave me a rabbit, a hare and a dozen eggs which will keep us for a week. We never seemed to stop talking for two days.

JANUARY 10TH

Jane and I ought to have caught the 11.27 bus to Platt to lunch with Denton Welch but through my carelessness in stopping to chat with Mary Jones we missed it.

The next bus only took us as far as Seal, so we stopped the first car we could see there. It kindly picked us up but the driver had just had an operation on her nose and was hurrying to get home before the cocaine wore off! We sat behind with her dog, Alice, and she took us to Ightham, which was at least beyond the policeman. We then walked in slushy snow against the N.E. wind towards Borough Green and I stopped two young Air Force officers, but they had to be at Maidstone by one o'clock so they could only take us as far as Platts Mills and we walked the rest of the way but arrived at Denton's not too late. We lunched off his 18thC china and glass and old silver: a sublime meal, with the sun pouring in on us and had a good chat over coffee. Denton amusing and gossipy as usual.

JANUARY 12TH

J and C busy writing an article for *The Chronicle* on 'The Oaks', the Sevenoaks Youth Club they have been instrumental in founding. In spite of the war this has been a very happy holiday with them. We are now quite used to sleeping all together in the old basement kitchen. Chris has his bed against the wall, Jane is in the china cupboard, H and I are in the middle of the room. Outside our door, under the basement stairs, are Mary and Jestyn Jones and baby Tom. The boiler fire hisses and crackles comfortably and Perkin the cat and Benny the dog take their pick of our beds. I understand now how it can be really companionable and pleasant to sleep in what I would once have thought of, in horror, as slum conditions, and how the poor little London evacuee children must *hate* sleeping alone when they have to!

JANUARY 14TH
Heard about the fire bomb damage at Shoreham yesterday. Preston Hill Farm has been destroyed and I fear some loss of life in the village.

JANUARY 19TH
An exhausting first week of teaching at Walthamstow Hall. I don't really know enough about the subjects I am teaching. This means much preparation. However I have enjoyed myself on the whole in an arduous and anxious fashion. Air raid tonight as usual.

JANUARY 25TH
Another week of school gone and I feel happier about being able to do the job, though it is always a relief when the end of a lesson comes and Friday evenings are glorious! It is terribly cold at school; since the building was bombed there seem to be a lot of cracks and holes that let in freezing air and of course there isn't much in the way of heating. I have enjoyed doing 'Ballads' with the 4th form (12–14 year olds). In order to bring home to them the communal and historical narrative character of ballads I set them on to making up a ballad about the bombing of Walthamstow Hall and together we produced the following contributions suggested enthusiastically from all over the room.

1. There was a school called Walthamstow
   In Sevenoaks town in Kent.
   And all the girls from roundabout
   To this good school they went.

2. It was a clear September night
   The moon cast shadows long.
   And all the girls in bed did hear
   The sirens wailing song.

3. The hum of engines overhead,
   The boom of guns below,
   They roused the wardens of this town
   Who did their whistles blow.

4. A Jerry from his plane did see
   A building large and fine;
   He pressed the button, down it came,
   A huge explosive mine!

5. Then cried a girl, 'What is that sound?
   I hear a mighty crash.
   Is it the heavens falling down?
   A Herculean smash!'

6. 'Oh who is hurt?' the wardens cried.
   'Come answer one and all.'
   'No one, no one,' they gladly cried,
   Not one throughout the Hall.

7. 'Oh come with us,' the wardens cried.
   'We'll show you billets fine.'

They hurried from those leaping flames,
A long dejected line.

8. Then to the Cornwall Hall they went
   In kindly neighbours' cars.
   And all they left behind them were
   Flames, leaping to the stars.

9. Then outspake bold Miss Ramsay.
   To all the girls around:
   'I'd love to tell old Hitler
   That we're all safe and sound!

10. We'll build our good school up again
    Better than e'er before,
    And we will learn more than we did
    Throughout this wicked war.'

We are all proud of our ballad.

FEBRUARY 9TH
The aconites are out in the garden and the catkins in the
woods. It seems strange and terrible not to welcome
the first signs of spring with joy. Yesterday evening we
listened to the Prime Minister. He was extremely good
– a clear, convincing summing-up of the war situation:
short hammer-like phrases varied with good rounded
periods and quotations from Byron and the Bible. He
thinks we are on the brink of invasion but have grounds
for hope and comfort and are far stronger than we were
last summer. We seem to be rushing through Libya.

FEBRUARY 10TH

A lovely spring-like day, the hills lilac-coloured in the sun. Miss Ramsay asked me to give lessons on Churchill's speech, so I referred to it shortly to IVB; did more about it with IVA and more still with the upper forms. Children very responsive. I wish I were clearer and more quick witted but I often feel a pretty inadequate teacher as far as actual brain power is concerned though I seem to interest them. Home to a nice chatty tea with Mary Jones and Chris. Everything quiet at night, exquisitely peaceful, which one feels is ominous indeed! Still, I am cheered by Churchill and our continued success in Italy. Just as I finished writing this the warning went, accompanied by Chris whistling merrily from the bathroom. However, nothing bad followed *here* at any rate.

FEBRUARY 14TH

St Valentine's day, the birds all singing as they should. Jane wrote what I think a good sonnet on St Valentine and the bombing.

'So spires are lost, their old complacent stones
Quickening an instant in funereal flame.
So the shocked century tenfold atones
For satiate possession, with such shame
So stuffed convention turns to nakedness.
But stay – this Valentine's no marbled urn.
A sonnet's small, why stretch it with distress?
Can any such delay my Saint's return?
No, nothing shatters Time's supreme estate
Nor anniversaries accommodate

Those blustering bombs, nor bombs shake one, fixed
  date.
So move the moments in their constancy,
So march the sun and stars across the sky.
So faithful thou, so firmly fond am I.

Sad news of damage done to Shoreham last night. A
great many fire bombs dropped – I suppose they were
trying for Fort Halstead. Some loss of life.

FEBRUARY 16TH

I got back to school after flu and felt rather shaky but
got through six periods and helped to entertain two
Governors at lunch. Everyone very kind, but more and
more staff going down with flu. I feel guilty about my
free weekend coming up, though luxuriating in the idea.

Started off the next day with H on our bikes with
night things strapped behind and soon got hot in spite
of the snow. Had our lunch at Ightham at The Town
House and then went on to Denton Welch. He was still
in bed at 2.30, but we were quite happy looking at all
his lovely things till he appeared. He insisted on giving
us an exquisite tea and coming with us on his bike
towards Malling as far as the cross roads. Acting on
instructions we took the road marked Strictly Private,
which led through the Park of Yates Court and came
suddenly on a lake. It was a deep metallic blue and the
bullrushes at its edge were pink and an alder full of red
catkins hung over it. Wild ducks were calling to each
other. We left it regretfully and pushed on to the road,
but found the way blocked by barbed wire and soldiers

from the Pioneer Force busy in part of a house which had had half its front blown off. The soldiers asked us why we had not seen the warning notice and we explained that we had come through the Park. They said they were working at an unexploded bomb in the road, but they allowed us to lift our bicycles over the barbed wire and proceed on our way. I thought how strange it was that we now take these things quite as a matter of course. We were not in the least surprised or alarmed.

We slept well at our little homely Inn, just around the corner from the historic and splendid 'Town House'. Our barmaid was wearing trousers – women are taking to them now because they are so convenient to slip on in air raids. I wonder if I shall ever get a pair. The next morning we had breakfast in bed, brought to us in our tiny room with our toes hanging out of the window – the best bloaters we had ever tasted in our lives.

APRIL 1ST – 8TH

Busy producing scenes from Cranford and 'She Stoops to Conquer' at school with various forms. Jane home and helping me with the costumes. I was pretty tired with fire watching till the early hours, but the plays went off better than I expected – the children loved them and thank goodness the holidays have now begun.

Germany has declared war on Yugoslavia. I only hope they will make a stand like Greece. Much saddened by hearing of Virginia Woolf's suicide.

APRIL 8TH

Holiday fire watching duty at school from 3 pm to 9 pm,
the time went quite quickly and eventually old Langford
from the Almshouses came to take over for me. His
comic scarecrow-like figure slowly shuffled down the
long passages and up the steps. I gave up trying to do
more than to get it into his head the relative positions
of the office, his sleeping quarters and the cookery room
where the food is kept, but he kept on taking the wrong
turnings. At last I left him and he had a poor night of
it I fear, with planes overhead most of the time. However
he was bursting with importance the next morning and
charmed with the air raid wardens who had made him
a cup of tea.

EASTER

A curious Easter, no eggs, no Church service. At school
for fire watching from 9 till 1 o'clock. H came for me
then and I took him round the empty buildings. Somehow an empty school building seems so peculiarly
empty. On Easter Monday I woke excited at the thought
of a whole day with H in the country again. Sky very
grey but we set off with our bikes and caught the train
to T. Wells and then biked to Lamberhurst via Bayham
Abbey which was full of troops. In fact troops were
everywhere and their tracks of rubbish, but gleams of
sun warmed us as we ate our lunch in Lamberhurst
churchyard. Bicycling back against a strong wind was
exhausting and rain poured down on our last lap. However it was a good day and we spent a peaceful sleepy

evening, H reading aloud Virginia Woolf's *Life of Roger Fry*.

APRIL 16TH

Dreadful raid on London last night. The planes were over us ceaselessly. H away. After the nightmare was over I crept out to a lovely healing sunny morning. Much damage done I fear.

APRIL 18TH

Off to Tufton with the children. Trains hopelessly upset. We got to Cannon St. and took a taxi to Waterloo, only to find the station closed. The children then took the bags on to Clapham Junction while I phoned H. We all managed to meet at Stewarts for lunch, outside Victoria (the approach to which was blocked). Monica Godfrey (an Oxford friend now teaching at Roedean) was to join us there. She arrived late and was tired, having spent the night in Kennington Tube station. We then had to take Chris's flute to Rudel Carter – no transport to be had so we walked in pouring rain. Tottenham Court Rd was mostly in ruins, Oxford Circus closed to all traffic, ruins and debris everywhere – it was like one of those bad dreams in which one tries to get somewhere and is constantly thwarted, but we eventually got back to Clapham Junction, found our bags and landed up in a crowded train for Winchester. We found the household at Tufton as usual.

1941

After inspecting the new cows, new land girls and new milking machine, Jane and I left for the parents and Devon, Chris staying on to help with the farm. We had an hour's wait at Salisbury and dashed to the Cathedral (my favourite of all Cathedrals). We played our usual game of alloting houses in the Close to ourselves and all our friends, this time finding an odd tiny 18thC one just suitable for Denton Welch. The Cathedral aisles were piled with mattresses. The train was very late and when we tried to get lunch in the dining car the attendant was so rude that he made J cry with rage. Passengers sympathized and said he had already had a row with an officer, people's nerves are on edge. The guard was heard to say, 'I dunno what's come over the passengers today – they're like a lot of orphans, don't know where they've come from or where they're going to.' But presently that same rude attendant came along especially to sell us tickets for a 4th lunch and at Sidmouth he took our bags and umbrellas and almost kissed me goodbye so he must have repented. Probably the poor fellow had had a bad night with the raid.

Found Dad much better than I had hoped and absolutely himself, only gentler and toned down a bit by illness. Mother also seems cheerful and in very good form. Poor Aunt Flo who is staying with them, was trying to listen to a Dvořák quartet at tea, but we were all talking. 'Hush!' she said, 'do be quiet, this is so beautiful.' 'Not so beautiful as my daughter's voice,' said mother. I mentioned critically a certain married couple: 'They see so little of each other,' I said. Mother: 'Perhaps it's as well!' Jane: 'Oh Granny, how cynical.' Mother:

'Well, I only want them to be happy!' Actually she herself seems more devoted to Dad than ever, often talking of how extraordinarily lucky she has been to be his wife! He dwells less in the past than she and is planning out world affairs after the war. Some of his suggestions are excellent. For the first time ever perhaps I was conscious that the inviolability of their faith inspired rather than annoyed me. How I envy them!

On the evening we arrived there was a rainbow and Jane and I went out in the garden to see it better. After the sordid desolation we had just left in London, it seemed a divine symbol, like Noah's rainbow after the flood. The light lit up the hills beyond with extraordinary radiance – to the left, the bank of trees; a brilliant green, stood out against black cloud. In front was a deep rich purple-red newly ploughed field. As we looked, three shining white swans flew out from behind the hills and under the rainbow. We thought at first they were planes, but then we saw the flap of the wings and their long outstretched necks. They were followed by a whole flock and we watched till they flew out of sight and the rainbow faded.

APRIL 26TH

My 43rd birthday. Chris got up early and made me a cup of tea and a huge pile of toast for breakfast. Nice letters and presents. Judith's letter from Canada had arrived early. Poor dear, I'm afraid that though everyone is kind and the baby well, she is longing to be back. In the morning I sewed while J read Hardy's *Trumpet Major* to me and after an early lunch we three set off for

T. Wells by bus. J wanted to do a quick sketch of a curious doorway, so C and I found a warm corner nearby at the entrance to one of the big houses facing the common and sat on the pavement there, very happy with our arms round each other's necks and causing much pleasure to lorry loads of soldiers continually passing and waving to us. We then went to see Freddie Bartholomew and Cedric Hardwick in 'Tom Brown's School Days'. H came back fairly early, tired but not too exhausted to play the family drawing game after supper.

The next day Jane went back to Oxford and I decided to have the day in London with her as C was having his friend Andrew over. We had a very good lunch for two and sixpence at D. H. Evans, which is still standing though John Lewis next door exists no longer, but London not so depressing as last week. Then we went to Shaw's 'Major Barbara' in which Robert Nicholls, Emlyn Williams and Miles Mallison were all excellent. Saw Jane off at Paddington and felt gloomy at her going and the end of the holidays.

MAY 4TH

School in full swing. Extra fire watching this term. Busy time correcting Free Place and Eleven + papers, an interesting but rather harrowing job and I got into a muddle over averaging marks! Jane has transferred herself from the Slade to the Central School (also evacuated to Oxford). She likes Bernard Meninsky so much as a teacher – that is the main reason for the change. The first day of double summer time and suitably warm.

SATURDAY MAY 8TH

First fire watching duty at school this term. Went at 5 pm and worked and chatted till supper, then we were just about to retire when the sirens went, so we sat by the fire in Miss Ramsay's room instead. Miss Ramsay appeared unusually resplendent in a scarlet dressing gown and handed round biscuits. The planes were low and there was some gun fire. Presently however the old fire watcher came in in a great state about what he thought was an incendiary bomb down the chimney. So we all turned out into a beautiful and brilliant night. It was clear and cold and the moon was huge, the searchlights incredibly lovely as were also the flares and flashes of gunfire. After a time we went in to thaw by the fire and ate chocolate. At 2.30 am we trailed off to bed. I had a camp bed in the little reception room by the front door and got some sleep between gunfire. The All Clear went at 5.30. Tried not to think about what was happening in London.

MAY 12TH

Last night part of the House of Commons and the Deanery and Dean's Yard were destroyed and the British Museum damaged and much damage done also in the City. So sleepy all day – Hal to lunch.

MAY 14TH

Extraordinary news of Hess, Hitler's deputy who has landed in Scotland in an aeroplane! Worried over German attack on Crete. Denton Welch to tea, he can be very sweet. Gave a talk on Refugees at school. It finished too soon but people seemed interested so I dare say it was all right.

JUNE 3RD

With H to a splendid National Gallery concert. Myra Hess and the Griller String Quartet playing Mozart and Brahms. Clothes rationing begun. Am doing Poetry Anthology with Upper IV and was interested to find that Wordsworth was by far the most popular. Shakespeare comes next but quite a long way behind!

WHIT WEEKEND

Bicycled with H to Rolvenden to stay the weekend there at the Parsonage Guest House. We rode over to Benenden to see the Moore family but found only Betty at home. She was as friendly as ever and growing fast. She said, 'If it hadn't been for the war I should have gone a long, long way off when I leave school, to Headcorn! (only about ten miles away!) She also said: 'I wish the war would end and then I might travel, I might come and see you at Sevenoaks!' Her mother came in and insisted on giving me 6 duck's eggs to take home. We found dear Walkhurst looking neat and full of flowers in the front garden but they (the tenants) have taken up the old rose bushes and the currant bushes were smothered in grass.

1941

SUNDAY, JUNE 22ND

Very hot. Arranged about fetching the hens. It will be a great help with rationing to have them. Germany declares war on Russia. What will this mean? To school for fire watching, but only had to stay for 2½ hours during which I profitably corrected exam papers and finished Richard Livingstone's book on the *Future of Education*. It is very hard to tell what is happening in Russia, but the Germans seem to have shot down a large number of planes. However the Russians appear to be fighting well and the nation to be wholehearted about it. It is hateful that Finland is fighting for Germany now.

Chris's prize-giving yesterday, but no parents or outsiders allowed (because of air raids). He had to go up four times, two prizes, the music cup for his house and to be introduced to the Governors. It was sad not to be able to be there. His last school report from the Headmaster, said 'A school career on which I shall always look back with the greatest pleasure. He has brought distinction on the school as well as himself and I am also very grateful for the many out of school activities in which he has been generally helpful.' Well anyway, next he has at least a year at Oxford – after that he will be called up and whether he will join the Air Force or choose some non-combative service with the Quakers we don't know and I am sure he doesn't yet either.

JULY 20TH

Fire watching at school all the morning – then to tea with the Bosanquets which I enjoyed very much. I like their little green dining room hung with David Cox water colours and I liked meeting Mr Bosanquet for the first time. He is nicer than I expected. He has rather a charming tuft of hair coming straight out of his nose at the top. Denton Welch there. Mrs B has bought one of his paintings – a pale delicate still life. Interesting talk.

JULY 21ST

Miss Ramsay told me this morning that Miss Curryer's mother had died and that she wanted to come back next term to her job here as English teacher, but that she (Miss R) had hopes of being allowed to keep me as well, as part-time teaching and part-time youth organizer (whatever that may mean). I said I was very doubtful if I'd be any good at organizing. She said solemnly, 'You can do anything you want to do!' I only wish that were even half true! As a matter of fact I've been teaching very badly lately. E. Bell caught me out over having added up her exam marks wrongly and A. Dain at an inaccuracy over Tennyson! But all is forgiven if not forgotten. Miss R said she had been doubtful about taking on a married woman with a family – I was in fact an experiment! But actually I think it has worked pretty well with me, for worries at home tend to get balanced by worries at school and kept in proportion and I am sure the children appreciate being taught by someone who has children of her own – indeed they have said so.

JULY 27TH

Our family fire watching night in the street. J and C
took the first watches but, like a fool, I couldn't get to
sleep then when I had the chance. Warning at 2 a.m.
just as I was going out to relieve Chris. I sat for a long
while on our door step. It was a lovely night – flashes
and planes busy, but no sound of bombs, only a very
loud swish once and a clatter, probably a big bit of shell
coming down, a dog howled dismally – the stars very
bright. Wrote this from about 3 a.m. to 4 a.m.

[*During August we were in the West Country visiting
relatives and my parents. By the end of the month I was
back in Sevenoaks and doing my bit of holiday fire watching
at night at school sleeping in one of the empty ghostlike
classrooms. Before the Autumn term began my father had to
come to London for an operation. Luckily there was a lull
in the air raids and my Mother came with him and stayed
nearby.*]

SEPTEMBER 2ND

To Mother's hotel where I waited for her to come in
from visiting Dad who is in University College Hospital
for the prostate operation. I listened to the voices of the
people asking for their keys, mail etc and at last came
my Mother's voice, so much sweeter and gentler than
any of them. She is better and less anxious about Dad
today, though still not quite herself. He is doing well
and Kenneth was with him this afternoon so I took
Mother to buy a nightdress at Bourne & Hollingsworth.
The contrast between the white cambric garment which
we managed at last to track down, with its high plain

collar buttoned at the throat (price seven shillings and sixpence) and the gloriously coloured frail chiffon creations which absolutely horrified her was comical. Travelled home with Mrs Ashbee whose house is full of WAAFs. She is worried at their boredom and lack of leisure occupations.

SEPTEMBER 4TH

To London to visit Dad. Walking along Tottenham Court Road and Oxford Street, it is curious to note how used one gets to seeing gaps and ruined houses and takes them for granted. Maples looks perfectly extraordinary, as though a giant had bitten a large piece off it. At U. C. H. found Dad finishing dressing and irrepressible, and Mother flustered and darting to and fro trying to pack. Both of them thrilled by the picture Jane had painted for him and Mother insisted on showing it to all the nurses and to the hotel people when we got back there! She is quite shameless. After lunch while they rested I went to the Soviet Exhibition at the Suffolk Galleries and then to see the Sickerts, which were fine.

SEPTEMBER 9TH

To school to see Miss Ramsay. She was very affectionate and kind. I am to teach one day a week at Bromley – 3 days a week at W. Hall and spend one day it seems doing odd jobs at the Army Depot in Wildernesse Avenue and thus satisfy the authorities. The Bromley school is a day continuation school and the girls there are mostly in jobs but have time off for further education. Relieved all is arranged but depressed later by Miss R ringing me up and pouring forth my timetable which sounded much too full of work! Lovely day so, shaking off dull care, caught bus with J to T. Wells, lay in the sun on the common, had a wonderful late lunch in the Pantiles and bought Mendelssohn's Letters for 4 pence at a second hand bookshop. Last day of the holidays.

SEPTEMBER 17TH
Started teaching at Bromley – catching the 8.15 bus. Talkative woman on the bus: 'Wasn't the sun lovely yesterday. I got up late and did my bit of washing, not a lot you know, just what I had to do, then I got out my deck chair and sat in the sun and oh I was happy! I sat on and on and presently the kids came home from school and said: "What's for dinner?" I haven't a notion I said, there's nothing in the house. So Sally said "Well never mind, I'll get some lettuce," so off she ran to the bottom of the garden and pulled some, and went across the road and bought some tomatoes and washed them and arranged them nicely in a bowl and then I bestirred myself and went and got some mint and chopped some spring onions and we got some of the bread I made yesterday and we had a lovely salad there, sitting in the sun. And then the kids went off again and believe it or not my dear, I sat on till half past three. I'd promised my husband to make a bread pudding. "Well," I thought, "that takes 4 hours so there goes my bread pudding, we'll just have to do without." People do talk to each other much more in trains and buses now and I

enjoyed her and by the time she finished I was at my stop.

The school is up a turning off the High Street and Bromley looked pretty knocked about, but the school bright and clean within and newly decorated. Suffered the usual agony at beginning anything new – a nightmare of strange faces. The staff seem very pleasant, but I was disconcerted at having to teach more classes than I had prepared. The younger girls are the most alive, the older ones will be a bit of a problem; they are obviously only attending because they must and grudge the time especially on such a subject as mine. I think drama is the thing for them – something fairly modern too.

SEPTEMBER 18TH

Good to be back at W. Hall today among all the familiar surroundings: the children and the staff I know so well. At staff meeting we had a lively discussion on hitch hiking, which is becoming common. Miss Ramsay defended it saying to our amused surprise that she herself had enjoyed hitch hiking from Shropshire (where the juniors are evacuated) stopping lorries without hesitation. I said I frequently gave lifts to people when I was going to and fro to Benenden – most of us agreed it made journeys more interesting.

OCTOBER AND NOVEMBER

I have been too busy to write much in this diary for some time.

Both my two are now settled in at Oxford. Chris has

joined a choir and orchestra, and Jane is enjoying
Bernard Meninsky's art classes. It was mainly because
of Meninsky that she left the Slade. I've taken on two
plays just now – one at W. Hall and one at Bromley.
Teaching goes well on the whole, though Bromley has
its difficulties. I see Denton Welch regularly as he comes
to Sevenoaks to take a voluntary art class with the Oaks
Youth Club. He was very excited last time as he had
sold some flower paintings at the Leicester Galleries. He
had met Lord Berners whom he described as taking
snuff incessantly from a gold snuff box and he is painting
his portrait. Judith arrived safely back from the States,
but left little Rachel behind with the Howells, the friends
she had made there. She felt she had to come back for
Richard's sake and also to do war work, but it was a
fearful wrench leaving the child and I fear she is eating
her heart out for her – though very glad to be in England
again. She was interesting about the classlessness of
American society; she says that money has taken the
place of class which she thought was even worse.

The War news is better from Russia and Libya, but
Japan has declared war and has attacked U.S.A. shipping
and has sunk 'The Prince of Wales' and 'The Repulse'.
All this in one week. Germany has declared war on
U.S.A. so almost the whole world is at war. This may
lengthen things considerably but if the German reverses
in Russia continue they may crack sooner than we
thought possible. For me, life could be so good now *if
it wasn't for the War* (a big IF). The twins both happy
at Oxford (life is enlivened by their charming letters), H
so dear, and work on the whole enjoyable. I feel almost
ashamed too, that during the past year I have had better

domestic help than ever before. Two North country sisters, Matty & Alice, pop in from their cottage in Six Bells Lane, three minutes away and cook and clean for me. They are both angels though very different. Matty, the elder has great dignity and intelligence – she is large and always serene and benevolent. Alice is small, round faced, with round blue eyes, twinkling with agitation. They come from Yorkshire, their father had been a farmer who had failed in the agricultural depression before the first world war, but Matty claims with pride, and I believe her, that they are direct descendants of Sir Isaac Newton. She says they had his Christening cup as a family treasure and has never forgiven Alice for parting with it to an antique dealer for ready money when they were hard up and she, Matty, was not by to stop her. Another of Matty's stories which I like tells how, when she was a child, the family were moving house. The village in which they were going to make their new home was some distance away and their father piled all their furniture into a cart and drove off – the children perched on top. It was winter and cold and as they came down a moorland road it began to snow. They were still some miles away from their destination but driving through the village of Lastingham they saw a cottage with a TO LET board. Her father drew up the pony, got down and there and then went to see the landlord. He came back with a key in his hand. 'As it's such a bad day and a cold journey,' he said, 'I think we'll stop here. So they unloaded the furniture, took possession and remained there for the rest of her parents' lives. What happened about the other cottage she did not know.

Alice was separated from a husband who is never

mentioned, but has three rather splendid sons, brought up by both sisters, two are now in the Navy and one in the Army. To Matty and Alice I owe the ease with which I have carried on my job and also therefore, much of its pleasure.

1942

JANUARY 18TH

Friends Meeting today in my house (the YWCA hut where we used to meet no longer available). There were eleven present, plus Perkin who likes attending meetings. Talk on starving Europe. Very cold. In the afternoon walked with Ben in Knole Park; the snow is thick after a heavy fall yesterday. When I left a bedroom window open, forgot it and went up later I found the bed and floor spread with a beautiful white cover! Secretly I rather enjoy this weather; I always feel well on dry, cold days and extremes (as long as they don't last too long) are exciting, only one mustn't think of the soldiers in Russia. In the Park there was that hushed winter stillness, the trees like skeletons, not a stir among the branches anywhere; the white roof showed up the black gables and griffons on the north side of Knole. A large group of deer were gathered in front of the building, as grey and as quiet as in an old print. The only movement was in little flocks of tits that were fluttering round the patches of beech leaves between the tree trunk forks.

In the evening there was a wonderful BBC programme. First Irene Scherer playing Chopin and then

Max Beerbohm on old Music Halls. He sang some bits of the old songs and invented others. Every word was perfectly clear. He told us that the author of 'Daisy, Daisy give me your answer do' wrote a song every day of the year! 'Not, I fear a strict Sabbatarian. He got paid one pound a song. I wonder if he said to himself: "Not marble, nor the gilded monument shall outlive this powerful rhyme." Good night children everywhere.' His intonation is sheer joy. Altogether one prayed for him never to stop. Nothing is so completely satisfying as intellect, wit, humour and a classic sense of form, added to which is the beauty of Max's voice. Jane and H loved it too and H got red in the face from trying not to laugh too much so as to drown any of it. I went to bed quite happy because of this broadcast and it coloured my dreams too.

FEBRUARY 9TH

The extreme weather has ceased to be in the least exciting. It is terribly cold at school and in all public buildings. In the bus to Bromley yesterday, the conductress fainted from the cold. When I got there I found no one had expected me because of the weather, but teaching the few who had turned up went well. On the other hand the 'Youth Community' evenings at Charlton House are deadly. No one knows what we are supposed to be doing there so nothing worthwhile gets done. We are reduced to mending huge piles of soldiers' socks, which is useful I suppose but not inspiring. Coming home in the dark and bitter fog the other night was blacker than black and I felt entirely helpless and had to stumble back and search miserably for help. At last I managed to secure the loan of a tiny feeble lamp and managed to avoid bumping into the mocking sightless lamp posts and the trunks of trees. Behind me a solitary dark car was hooting its way at a snail's pace up the hill.

MARCH 4TH

It has turned bitterly cold again with N.E. wind and snow. Went to hear E. M. Forster lecture on Virginia Woolf at the Royal Institute. He is rather a droopy and sandy-coloured man, but, once he begins to speak, impressive in a quiet way and what he had to say was illuminating and compelling. He said 1942 was not a good vintage year for judgement – that his subject was too rich – Virginia Woolf was like a plant, springing up in all sorts of unexpected places, sending out suckers which thrust up in courtyards and kitchens as well as in gardens. She wrote because she liked writing – not to earn money, not to make the world a better place, not to add to her repute and this was unusual. She was concerned with one thing only – writing. How then did she avoid falling into the depth of the Palace of Art? By humour. She was always aware when she was getting bored or boring – as in the latter part of Orlando. He then dealt with all her books individually, finishing with the two last, *Flush* and the biography of Roger Fry. He said the biography was like a classical musical composition with theme, development, variations and summing up. In *Flush*, (Elizabeth Browning's spaniel) which might have been disastrously 'doggie', but was not so, 'we learn from the level of the sofa new lights upon the great.' 'From Flush to Roger Fry – I am sure Fry would not mind and spaniels never mind anything.' In a summing up which I thought very valuable in the light of her suicide, he said 'She was tough with an admirable hardness, sympathy was not easy to her, for it meant adding other people's troubles to one's own and one thought twice about that. If people thought too much about the sorrows of others, no houses would be built, no roads made, no books written, only one long wailing cry would go up to heaven.' He finished by saying that: 'Nothing is here for tears', her life was a triumphant achievement – she worked hard and produced much beauty – 'it was a series of silver cups, trophies won by the brain in spite of the body'. I suppose it is too soon to assess her, but I think that probably she and E. M. Forster himself have had more influence on me than any other contemporary writer except perhaps Shaw but he really belongs to an earlier period.

APRIL

The Easter holidays have passed, mostly filled with fighting illnesses in the family of various kinds. Little war news. It is a bleak spring, still cold at school. A meeting at the Chantry on Europe was well attended and the speaker, Alison Wood, clear and informative. The state of occupied Europe is sad and depressing, difficult to realize, little education and what there is is false, no travelling, even in urgent cases, shortage of everything, no room in the hospitals, fear increased by constantly changing rules and regulations, degradation of women between the ages of 15 and 45 legalized and liable to imprisonment if they refuse. And yet, through it all a new unity, the barriers of sects and classes gone, little anti-semitism, only sympathy.

On my birthday picked marsh marigolds and bluebells and pink campion with H. I wish there was a quite new adjective to describe the beauty of spring flowers.

MAY 16TH

Breakfasted alone. H home soon after, having worked all night, but he did not seem tired and as it was a lovely warm day at last we took the bus to Otford and then walked to Shoreham through the Park – the lower footpath was closed. We waded through the buttercups and the whole village looked utterly peaceful and delightful. We had not been there since the first big air battle over London. Samuel Palmer's house (Water House) is for sale, the two old bachelors who lived in it when we first knew it having both died. We went over it for curiosity's sake. It is a very pleasant, sober, comfortable house with wide square-panelled rooms, austere, good and perfectly kept furniture, Whistler etchings on the walls. Everything is just as the last old gentleman had left it, even to his brushes laid out on his dressing table. A dignified and rather beautiful housekeeper showed us round; she had been there twenty years. Outside is the old walled garden full of fruit trees (one of which may be the Apple Tree painted by Palmer) neat flower beds and grass paths, not much variety or individuality in house or garden but very English, unostentatious, solid, comfortable and gracious.

On to the White Cottage, where comely Mrs Barker

in handsome gold earrings and large brooch made us welcome. The shadowy silent elderly man, whom she always calls 'Uncle,' at her side as usual. She has given up providing teas and Uncle is now living in part of the cottage. What vicissitudes we have known at that cottage. Dad cajoled Mrs Barker into taking them in there for a holiday in 1931, and we four stayed there between our move from Otford to Sevenoaks in 1938. [*The cottage was completely destroyed by a flying bomb in 1944.*] The long garden, more charming I think even than Water House garden, reaches right up to it and the cottage must often have been seen by Palmer. Home to supper and then slipped in next door to see Mary with her new baby. She is pretty well but had rather a nasty time. They have asked Chris to be his godfather.

JUNE

The news this week has been of an enormous raid on Cologne involving over 1,000 of our bombers. Great damage done. Even if this is necessary, which is most doubtful, I *hate* the way it is given out, the gloating over it and especially Churchill's congratulatory threat. A reprisal raid on Canterbury has taken place and we are not allowed to know whether the Cathedral has been hit. It is said the Cathedral at Cologne is safe. A new attack on Rommel seems to have held. Neither side are making much progress in Russia. Heydrich has died of his wounds and over 200 Czechs have been executed in revenge. [*Heydrich was Gauleiter in Czechoslovakia.*] And the June days and nights so lovely here! We are sleeping out at the top of the garden behind the shed and between two and three a.m. last night I felt a hand touching my blanket which woke me. I turned round and saw an enormous strange man looming between me and the stars. Almost at once I realized that he was a policeman. H had left the attic light on in the house and there was a chink in the blackout. The policeman of course could get no answer and had roused both our neighbours; Jestyn Jones had told him to come up the garden. He was quite nice about it and H went in to extinguish the light. In the morning the poplars the other side of our wall are floodlit by the rising sun. Birds' wings swish over us.

Chris is doing 'Mods' (maths) this week and doesn't seem to have liked the papers much but I expect he's alright. He worries me though by a wild project to spend the vac filling shells and being medically experimented on instead of working on the farm at Tufton. His health isn't too good and I wish he were more sensible about it.

JULY

To Tufton to see Madeleine, trains crowded as usual. Little Rob is a bewitching child; with huge brown eyes and red curls and an enchanting smile. He is interested in everything and sometimes terrifyingly impatient! His world is a most exciting one. I find it most comforting nowadays to be with small children. It is hay harvest and B has Italian prisoners working in the fields. They look lovely and seem happy and friendly and I don't think they have ever been very warlike! On the way home I stayed one night with Ellen in Hampstead where she now is living, having let Crouch Farm House. She was eager to show me her childhood's home at the top of North End Road – a tall late Georgian house, rambling and gaunt and now bombed and covered with broken glass below. We climbed all over it and saw Ellen's little bedroom where she had slept from three years old upwards, still a pleasant little room, the roses coming in through the smashed window. Next door the house had been razed to the ground; a peacock was picking its way delicately among the ruins. These houses are on the edge of the Heath over which we then walked through the silver birch grove where Ellen had conducted four love affairs and had had three proposals, and had climbed trees by moonlight with Dr Horton (the congregational minister who had christened all our family!) The grove was quite deserted. We walked right up to the pond where my sister and brother used to sail their boats, myself looking on from my pram, and past Filton House. Said goodbye to Ellen and went on by tube and met H and then he and I walked again through sordid, hot, bombed streets and then suddenly turned into the wide and faded magnificence of Chester Gate and the Park. We were making for the British School of Architecture, once St John's Lodge, a fine Regency building with a vista in front of statues and vases fit for a palace – it had been built as the private home of a John Maberly Esq. At the doorway stood Mrs Seligman, lovely as usual, in green silk, piled grey curls and a wide green hat. A little Chinese lady, Madame Kuo, was to talk to us. We had a war-time tea which *looked* lovely but which tasted of nothing. Mme Kuo was tiny in a wonderfully embroidered dress and she made all the Western ladies look gross and fussy. She arrived late on purpose, to secure her audience and spoke with great assurance on women in China, then educational influence and financial ability and war effort – told of an old woman of seventy who had her own band of guerilla warriors and had three times escaped from prison. After her a quiet student spoke of the need for help in modernizing education in China.

It was good to get back home for a quiet evening alone with H again. I am reading Wesley's Journal and he and I are reading Shaw's and Ellen Terry's love letters aloud to each other – a good mixture.

JULY 26TH

A restful day after stress of end of term. All went off well, including, surprisingly, the production of 'The Rose and the Ring' with the boys (most of them London evacuees). They *have* been a headache – cutting rehearsals or else turning up very late, never knowing their parts etc. etc., but rather sweet through it all and coming up to scratch marvellously on the night itself. Never shall I forget Graham's look of incredulous pleasure when the curtain went down after the first act. 'It's a success,' he whispered, 'but I haven't come on yet though!' Anyway everyone was pleased and Peggy and I (joint producers) very relieved.

Today I gardened and read and H and C played duets in the evening, everything cheerful at home but the news isn't good from Russia, better from Egypt.

[*The Germans were pressing Russia hard but in Egypt*

Montgomery was beginning to hold his own against Rommel.]

JULY 28TH
Fought down panic feelings of despair at Germany's strength and went to meet Ethel (Ginsberg) in the Green Park where we sat among the barbed wire and dugouts and discussed life. She is bored with housework and wants to take up psychiatric work, I think influenced by Dr Miller [*Father of Jonathan Miller.*] We walked to Hyde Park Corner meeting nothing but poodles. Then we went to the film of the Young Mr Pitt. Disappointingly sentimental with a travesty of Charles James Fox. H away. Chris came home early to be with me and we talked till the small hours.

AUGUST BANK HOLIDAY
Sat by our open sitting room window looking onto the High Street. There were a few motor bikes, no cars, some horses and carts and a great many people walking quietly past. Bottled fruit and made carrot marmalade out of carrots and orange skins. Madeleine sent us some salmon which has fed us for three days! Jane arrived yesterday at tea time from Yorkshire – without her luggage which had been left at Charing Cross! She had started at 5.30 a.m. She was very full of Friends Meeting at York and had met the Heu family there, Berti, she said, looked much older, pale and thin and with the cares of the family on him, poor little boy. Prof. and

1942

Mrs Heu and Christoph and Berti all talked at once to her without reference to one another!

AUGUST 15TH

To London for the day. First I got tickets for 'Othello' and then met H at National Gallery and we went to Lincoln's Inn to see the Inigo Jones houses, now inhabited by a branch of the Patent Offices. Mr Trigg received us and is very kind and courageous. He presented us with a history of Lincoln's Inn Fields. His room contained very good mouldings and an original mahogany desk which had been blown out of the house by a bomb explosion, but hardly damaged. This room was that in which Lord Russell's body was carried after his execution. We also saw the room in which Dickens used to read aloud to his friends. Mr Trigg told us of all the precautions he had taken to preserve this room from bomb damage. He himself had had some narrow escapes. He showed us a talisman of ancient yew wood that he always carries about with him. He said, 'I touch it not through superstition but through humility.' H and I walked about 'The Fields' which look very attractive and rather continental without their railings then I met Jane at Charing Cross. It was terrifically hot and there were very long queues for meals at Lyons Corner House, so we went to Leicester Square and had a nice supper at the 'American Restaurant' and all went well until it was time to pay my bill when I found that because I had bought a book at the National Gallery I had not enough money left. Frantic searchings through Jane's bag produced only half the amount needed. The waitress, however, was angelic, she said, 'I can see that you are an honest woman,' and refused even to take my name and address. The man at the desk just said 'Have you enough to get home?' I believe in a moment they would have pressed a loan on us. Such an experience is worth the agony of being short of money. 'Othello' was good, especially Frederick Falk the Czech actor. Freda Jackson as Emilia was excellent, what a marvellous character! Desdemona, Hermione Hannan, had her moments, but was not helped by a costume like Britannia. Jane wept throughout the last act. We travelled home with Mr and Mrs Rich. I said, 'Have you by any chance been to "Othello"?' Mr Rich said, 'Yes, we have! No, we haven't, we've been to "Macbeth"!' H in town for the night. I slept out alone – a lovely night.

AUGUST 25TH TO SEPTEMBER 5TH
In Devon staying at Sidmouth to be near the parents. Dad very well, Mother always sweet and herself, but sometimes distressingly vague, but it was a refreshing time on the whole. H only able to get away for a few days, but Jane and Chris with me all the time. Chris, a much better knitter than either J or myself, pleasing Mother very much by knitting up the soldier's scarf with which she was struggling. Among some of her old papers she found the following Table Rules from her first school. I suppose the date to be about 1869.

In silence I must take my seat
And give God thanks for what I eat,
Must for my food in patience wait

Till I am asked to pass my plate.
I must not scold or whine or pout,
Nor move my chair or plate about.
I must not speak a useless word
For children should be seen not heard.
I must not talk about my food
Nor fret if I don't think it good.
I must not say: 'the bread is old,
The tea is hot, the coffee cold.'
My mouth with food I must not crowd,
Nor while I'm eating speak aloud.
The table cloth I must not spoil.
Nor with my food my fingers soil.
Must keep my seat when I have done,
Nor round the table sport or run.
When told to rise, then I must put
My chair away with noiseless foot,
And lift my heart to God above
In praise for all His wondrous love.

My Mother certainly wouldn't have kept these rules to the letter! She was rather a naughty, merry little girl who got into trouble for mimicking the teachers.

On the third anniversary of the outbreak of the war we went down to a fine rough sea immediately after breakfast. The huge glistening waves, the red cliffs, the gulls and the R.A.F. band playing as they marched along, was enough to put spirit into anyone. We went to the special service, the church was packed. We looked very unchurchlike, I had no stockings and no hat, J was in her old red trousers and Chris in shorts. The sermon had no merit except brevity.

1942

The journey home was horrible, very slow and crowded. There was a child in the train from London to Sevenoaks, looking out of the window and chanting 'that house has been bombed, that house hasn't been bombed, that house has been bombed, that house hasn't been bombed.' I'm afraid I hate the holidays coming to an end.

NOVEMBER 5TH – DECEMBER 31ST

News from Egypt very good. [*The victory of El Alamein, one of the turning-points of the War.*] If this could be an overwhelming victory it might be the beginning of the end. H and I went to the film, 'The First of the Few', Leslie Howard's good film about Mitchell – the Spitfire designer and the Battle of Britain. It was extremely interesting and if aeroplanes *had* to be invented and, still more, if a war *had* to come then the genius of Mitchell was invaluable to us. This film could not help moving anyone, I should think, who had lived through 1940 with thanksgiving at the country surviving against such odds. Grand news coming now, French North Africa successfully invaded by American troops. Roosevelt has appealed to the French to cooperate. Rommel's retreat goes on. Went to see perfect production of 'The Importance of Being Ernest' with Gielgud, Peggy Ashcroft, Edith Evans and Gwen Franklyn Davis. Horrid foggy journey home but dear H had wanted to travel home with me so waited for him. In the train were two ladies, one had had to fly home from Rangoon and all her furniture, which was in store, had been bombed, the other had had her house in Canterbury completely destroyed and a cottage in Kent. She added almost apologetically 'It is rather tiresome, isn't it.'

Churchill's Mansion House speech said, 'A gleam has shone on the helmets of our soldiers and warmed all our hearts.' What has also warmed *my* heart is that H has been awarded the platinum medal for 'outstanding scientific services in non-ferrous metal research' – the highest honour given. Madeleine and little Rob to stay. He is a beautiful child and very intelligent, but tiresome over food. Anthea has also been for a visit, looking thin but seeming happy.

Worried and sad about John Falk and Skepper, both prisoners in Japanese hands. The Japs have put up a notice 'Prisoners are not to look too happy or too sad.'

CHRISTMAS DAY

A quiet and strained Christmas with Kenneth and the two children here [*my sister-in-law had died suddenly of heart trouble recently*]. Chris is so good with young John [*my nephew aged 14*]. Jane has decided to leave the Central School and do war work with the Friends. This involves helping at an old people's home (mostly evacuees) at Gristhorpe in Yorkshire.

DECEMBER 31ST

Little Betty Moore from Benenden is now nursemaid to Mary, next door – thus fulfilling her dreams of travelling, and today Chris is taking her to London (her first visit) as my Christmas present to her: I hope it won't completely turn her head! They are going to St Paul's, Selfridges and the Pantomime. They went off looking so young and appealing, he in his outgrown overcoat and red muffler and she sporting a little sealskin muff that had belonged to her mother. She is the most innocent and simple of creatures and adores him quite openly, but utterly romantically as a sort of god – and I know that he is too wise and kind for it to do her any harm. J and I bought grey jersey and dungarees to fit her out for Yorkshire – then walked in a snowy pink Knole for an hour and after tea (mince pies and Russian tea) settled down happily, she to write reviews for Cyril Connolly's 'Horizon' and myself to read. Neither of us wanted anything else to happen ever. I have longed lately more *than ever* for the war to end. Darlan has been conveniently assassinated – the Russians seem to be doing well, but ourselves not quite so well now in Africa. [*Admiral Darlan was controller, under Hitler, of the French possessions in North Africa.*]

1943

[*This was a comparatively quiet year in England as far as air attacks went. The chief menace in the early months was from submarines and the Merchant Navy was badly hit, but food rationing was effective and no one suffered as I remember they had done in the First World War. Food was dull but adequate and healthy. There is therefore comparatively little war news recorded in my diary for this period. But it was a sad time for our family. Judith contracted cancer which rapidly proved fatal. This was almost certainly a result of the war. She was a very loving person and the parting from her home and husband and family in order to take her baby to safety in America was terrible for her. Then the decision she took to come back to continue the war research work in Oxford, leaving the baby behind in the States, was a no less terrible strain. Her deep unhappiness, suppressed by unselfish courage, for she never complained, was I feel sure, a main contributing cause of her cancer . . . I shall only give brief entries from the Diary upon this private sorrow.*]

JANUARY 22ND – 30TH

End of holidays alas! – saw Jane off and miss her greatly, but cheered by very good concert at Walthamstow Hall – the Griller string quartet playing Haydn, Schubert and Dvořák. All Sevenoaks seemed to be there, exchanged greetings from all over the Hall including many relations as well as friends. This same week I have been moved by the film that I saw with H about the Navy: 'In Which We Serve' and by a very good and heart-warming meeting on Famine Relief; also by reading Richard Hillary's book *The Last Enemy*, and Dick Sheppard's life. I have read too with much interest *Last train from Berlin* which made me feel desperately sorry for most of the German people. Margaret Godfrey's husband has been made Commander of the Indian Fleet and she is going out to Delhi in May. She thinks the Japs will go on fighting for a long while but I don't – not with the continued forces of Great Britain, China, U.S.A. and possibly Russia against them.

FEBRUARY 12TH

Weather warm, wet and wild. Many trees down in Knole Park. Rushed morning, then at 1.30 to Famine Relief shop. Depressed at first hour as no one came in. It is frustrating to see them passing negligently by, but things gradually cheered up as the afternoon wore on. Elizabeth Buxton to tea, looking weather-beaten but kind and firm as usual with her nice greeny-hazel eyes and low voice. She and her father, aged 88, live in the dining room of that huge house (Fairfield at Hildenborough) with the ancient butler and cook and the two old aunts at Tunbridge Wells. Saddened by news that Adrian Seligman's ship is lost.

FEBRUARY 25TH

To tea with the Cummings family for Dorothy's birthday. Barbara was there with little Roger. He was busy with bricks when D kissed him on the back of his neck. 'Don't do that,' he said, annoyed at being distracted, but immediately after he turned and added: 'Nice of you to kiss me though.' Not bad for under three years old. Barbara was very nice and dear.

MARCH 3RD

To London for H's luncheon party and the meeting of the Institute of Metals afterwards. Wore my plum-coloured coat and skirt (nearly new) and grey fur hat. I had this good material made up by my not very good dressmaker and it doesn't look smart I fear, but saved a lot of clothes coupons and the colour is nice. At the Hotel was met by Sir John Greenly; Dr Desch and dear Dr Seligman and was so delighted to hear that Adrian is safe. The luncheon went off very well though H never said a word throughout! Afterwards I walked in the Park with Seligman and discussed the German character. He is gloomy about Russia. Then it was time to go to the meeting. Sir John was very nice about H – his integrity, modesty, transparent sincerity (as well as brains of course!) and H made a good speech in reply though with rather long pauses due, I know, to emotion but not noticeable I think to anyone but me.

[The rest of the month was taken up by illness – both H and myself down with flu and Jane ill at Birmingham where she was now working. (This was also a very sad time as we now were told of Judith's cancer.)]

APRIL 3RD

Broke up thankfully. In evening went to the Chantry to meet Col. Ponsonby MP. We were eight women and eight men. We asked him questions about the Beveridge Report, Famine relief – Russia, Jewish refugees and Sunday cinemas. He showed himself ill informed about Famine Relief and the Jews and read us an entirely irrelevant report from the Ministry of Economic Warfare; the whole thing too stupid. He wasn't too bad on the Beveridge Report though poor on children's endowments. Altogether he appeared charming, courteous and slippery. But it does show merit to meet us at all and he has promised to look into things and meet us again.

The U-Boat campaign against our Merchant Shipping is now very serious.

APRIL 4TH

Jane home on sick leave. She told lovely stories of the old ladies at Gristhorpe, one of them called Emily Crackles has sent her a medal blessed by the Pope and with a letter 'Just a few lines to thank you for your many deeds of kindness and comforting words and reading to me you was always willing to do anything for me and did it with a smile when you was on the staff of Gristhorpe, Yorkshire. I thank you dear and wish you the best of luck wherever you go from an evacuee from Hull. God bless you and watch over you, keep smiling all through. XXXX Emily Crackles.' Oh dear I wish I hadn't got to go and stay at Lyme Regis with Ellen just now and leave my family, but I promised long ago to join her at her cottage there for a few days. Food parcel received from Judith's friends in America. Great excitement – a lovely tinned chicken and most useful coffee, but the chocolate which excited us greatly at first was a sad disappointment. It had suffered during transit, was grey and tasted horrid!

APRIL 7TH

This old coastguard's cottage is very attractive. Ellen has painted it black and white, symbolic of good and evil as she characteristically informed me! The flowers here are wonderful, big pink poppies and peonies already in bud side by side with daffodils, lilac, wallflowers, bluebells and cowslips and yet the blackthorn still in flower and the great trees still bare.

Today we called on Tony Birrell (Augustus Birrell's son) and Miss Tattersall, his cousin who lives with him. Their house is charming – big eighteenth century windows looking right across to Charmouth Bay – the further cliffs were lit up by a fitful sun. The sitting room overflowing with books and portraits, caricatures of Victorian authors: [*the Birrell family were connected with Tennyson*] all so nostalgic and peaceful. The garden, full of aromatic shrubs, has a view of the Cobb. Tony is a simple, kindly, hapless man; Miss Tattersall vigorous and amusing. Although homesick for H and cross at

missing Jane who has to get back to Birmingham as soon
as possible, I am enjoying the beauty of Lyme, the
huge primroses and brilliant gorse and bluebells on the
Undercliff. I walked there by myself and picked a bou-
quet for Ellen of fourteen different kinds of wild flowers.

APRIL 9TH – 12TH

With the parents on my way home and saddened by old
age. Mother is losing her memory but her sweetness
and love remain unchanged. She is so selfless, she kept
reverting to how blessed she had been in life and still is
– how lucky to be at 'Long Range' (this guest house),
never a word of complaint at having to give up her own
home. As usual I was cross and argumentative with Dad
but was better on the second day and I enjoyed another
walk by myself past Larkbeare House, Charles Kings-
ley's old home, the door was open and a maid was
polishing the brass knocker and a small boy was playing
among the daisies on the lawn – what peace! Going home
I took a track which led to a dark little pine wood,
through the tree trunks was an edging of bright green
corn. A large tawny owl swept silently past me. I broke
my journey home again to see Judith. The day after,
Chris phoned from town to ask me to come up and go
with him to see Congreve's play but I didn't feel up to
it, afterwards regretted this because of disappointing him
but he arrived at 8 o'clock not at all reproachful. It is
so nice to have a child at home again. Reading *Northanger
Abbey* aloud to H in the evenings – very soothing.

MAY 8TH

Back at school – lessons went all right but perishingly cold there and I was very glad to come back to a fire. News good – Bizerta and Tunis have both fallen. This brings our invasion nearer which is terrifying yet necessary for the end. Madeleine came with little Rob. He remembered everything. Papers are full of rounding up the enemy in Africa. Got Denton's book *Maiden Voyage*. I am so glad for him that it is safely out under Edith Sitwell's wing. How well I remember sitting with him in his little car at Borough Green waiting to meet Ellen and his asking me about how to approach publishers etc.

JUNE 12TH TO 16TH

At Oxford for half term, staying at the Eastgate Hotel with H. Our room looks out on Magdalen Tower. Went to Friends meeting with Chris who afterwards punted me up the Char and landed me in the Parks from whence I rushed across to Judith and Richard's flat arriving late because it took more time on the river than we thought and Chris fell in as I got out! He is very good and nice but a bit wild at times! He took us to an interesting meeting of the Socratic Club of which he is secretary. John Macmurray and C. S. Lewis both spoke. Macmurray I thought was the better of the two. He was anti-dualist. 'Belief and Action are one not two.' 'Nature and supernatural are modern romantic terms – misleading in their duality.' C. S. Lewis appeared unhappy and rather aggressive as though he couldn't bear to be disagreed with at all.

JULY 6TH

A pleasing short interlude today when I went with Mary to Farningham to see the Manor House where she used to stay with the Alberys, a lovely old red brick house, now a mass of ruins from the 1940 bombs, except for one wing. We had tea on the banks of the Darenth and then drank another cup with the caretaker who lives in a cottage looking out on a perfectly peaceful and immaculate courtyard among the ruins with a green lawn and a procession of great, grey geese waddling majestically across it.

JULY 20TH

Prize Day and breaking up over and off to stay at Abingdon so that I could visit Judith. Everything at North-court House rather dreary and uncomfortable compared with the past, the food is awful. They simply don't know how to cope with rations and none of them care about food anyhow so have no imagination in dealing with it. But I am very thankful to them for having me just now and comforted to be with Evelyn.

AUGUST 28TH

(Judith died this morning. H and I were both with her.)

SEPTEMBER 1ST TO 24TH

[*This was a quiet time at home, doing household jobs, picking fruit, making jam etc. The twins were both with us until Christopher went off. Having had two years at Oxford (he*

*had had a year's deferred war service and hoped to return
ultimately to do his finals) he now was given a commission
in the R.A.F. and went to work at Airforce Operational
Research at Watford (later at Stanmore). Soon after he had
gone I began teaching once more and Jane went off to work
again too.*]

I found sympathy and special kindness at school, and
Miss Ramsay is letting me have a week off at the end of
the month so that H and I can go away together as we
were unable to do so in the summer. We have decided
to go to Yorkshire to the village of Lastingham, our
dear Matty and Alice's old home and they have strongly
recommended 'The Blacksmith's Arms' there. War news
from Italy encouraging. Thank goodness Mussolini is
finished off anyway. [*After Mussolini's downfall the new
Government signed an armistice with the allies.*]

SEPTEMBER 24TH

Started for Yorkshire. We had sent most of our luggage
in brown paper parcels by post so were able to travel
light as we were taking our bicycles with us, making us
feel a little less guilty at the admonition 'Is your journey
really necessary?' Cycling from Charing X to Kings X
was pleasant and easy. I think I shall remember coasting
the whole length of Gower Street at a good round pace
without a stop – no traffic to speak of. Journey uneventful to York where we stayed the night. It was raining in
York and we bicycled round trying to find accommodation and landed up in a tall gaunt house overlooking
a railway siding and kept by a tall gaunt woman with a
lame leg and an only son in Cairo. She showed us a

rather doubtfully clean bed with a dead plant in the window, but we took the room as it was late. Sausages and mash and a walk round the Minster cheered us up.

SEPTEMBER 25TH

On to Scarborough. Here we bicycled along South Cliff. The hotels are filled with the Air Force, the sea front was deserted. We passed the tattered and faded ruins of the Aquarium and the pleasure booths, past the brave old scarred Victorian lodging houses and then up Castle Hill where we ate the hard-boiled home-laid eggs that we had brought with us, our backs against the wall looking out at a rough peacock-coloured sea. It was a fitfully bright day. We saw what looked like a convoy, also some queer, stationary ships, brilliantly painted in white – what they were we could not guess. We took a little country train to Pickering and from there bicycled to Lastingham, the road getting wilder and steeper as we neared the village (Matty had warned us to ride carefully down Cropton Bank!) the sun set as we came over the bridge and it was dusk when we reached the Blacksmith's Arms and were welcomed by Mr and Mrs Crosby, the proprietors. In the sitting room, which we are to have to ourselves, there was a leaping glowing fire, two old comfortable arm-chairs, a rocking chair, a corner cupboard, a round table with geraniums in the window and a square table in the centre laid for supper. And in came a vast pigeon pie, potatoes and cauliflower, home-made cake and a big pot of tea. No war-time meal this!

I want now to put on record those pleasant people who helped us on our journey through Yorkshire – the

kind old porter who took our bicycles all across the
station at York; the little friendly fat, black lady at the
café, the postman who pushed our bikes back again
to the Scarborough platform, the particularly attentive
waitress who brought us tea, the countryman opposite
us in the train who cleared off his luggage to make room
for us and caught a bee that was worrying me and put
it out of the window, the patient shop-assistant at Pickering who actually managed to produce a pair of black
woollen stockings for me that I mean to send to my old
aunt. There is no doubt about it – these Yorkshire people
are more helpful and friendly than most Southerners.

SEPTEMBER 26TH

A very ample breakfast (home-cured ham) – apparently
unlimited butter and eggs here. Afterwards we went out
to explore. The moor comes down almost to the cottage
back gardens – the heather is over, only an occasional
purple clump remains but the pinky-brown colour of the
withered flowers and the bracken, just turning, provide
more varied and subtle shades than the full bloom. Along
the margin of the moors we walked to Hutton le Hole
and sought out plain, friendly, capacious 'Barmoor' [*the
home of the Quaker Harvey family*] well known to us by
repute from Jane and Sally Harvey's description. Hutton
is a cheerful village, facing all ways with a beck, a long
hummocky green, handsome intelligent-looking sheep
with polished black legs and faces and soft long grey
coats, tall hairy pigs and crowds of clean wandering and
happy hens. Home to roast beef and yorkshire pudding,
blackberry tart and cream and coffee. They really don't

seem to know anything about rationing here, the food is unbelievable. Walked again on the moors – no planes, no soldiers, no convoys, no tanks – the air and the peace extraordinarily invigorating. In the evening old Mrs Crosby came and talked to us, a dignified and acute old lady. She had known Matty well. She was a little melancholy over her past life – her husband had been in the Merchant Service and she had had a hard time; she had lived most of her life at Whitby. On the landing there is a beautiful old grandfather clock decorated with paintings of shells and of seaweed; it was made at Whitby over two hundred years ago and has always belonged to a John Crosby.

SEPTEMBER 30TH

The 21st anniversary of our wedding day and as perfect weather as we had for the day itself. We set out to bicycle to Kirby, Helmsley and Riveaux. At Kirby we decided that the church was not worth a visit but an irate and sinister-looking woman with wild black hair and no teeth emerged from a nearby cottage and more or less forced us to go in. We were right in our guess. At Helmsley the ruined castle would have pleased me once but I have seen too many ruins since the Blitz. Riveaux was glorious though and the Abbey did not give me that miserable feeling that ruins now produce because, like Fountains, it seems complete as though the green aisles and the windows and roof of blue sky had been planned like that. It is now a perfect fusion of nature and architecture. A beautiful ride home through Hutton, and then another magical un-warlike meal: roast chicken and cheese souffle and afterwards reading *Emma* aloud by the fire.

OCTOBER 1ST

A warm grey day but with breaks in the cloud and gleams of light. So warm it was, that I decided to sketch and did so with great pleasure and though not at all satisfied with the result yet not in despair. I spent some time chatting with Mrs Sunley at the village school, a friendly ginger-haired woman with a goitre. She was pleased to talk about Matty and Alice. H meanwhile had gone for a walk and picked up an aged Archdeacon whom he brought back with him. The bond was that he had once been Vicar of Middlesbrough, H's childhood home. He was a noble-looking old man with a nice smile; not literary I should think but loving the countryside. He called us 'my dears' and invited us to tea.

OCTOBER 2ND

A glorious day, perfectly cloudless blue sky and the moor glittering with light and colour, rooks scattering over the golden expanse. We decided to go to Whitby by bicycle and train. The train journey from Pickering to Whitby was most beautiful but the town itself had an air of shabbiness and desolation. The old tall red houses were dirty and had tiles missing from the roofs and the Victorian houses on the West Cliff were all peeling. We found the church locked and the Abbey closed to the public. A large and lovely but desolate eighteenth-century house and barn near the ruins of the Abbey completed the impression of past glories and present decay; the whole place was covered with WAAFS and ATS. Back by bus to Pickering and a good ride home with a little new silver moon rising over the dark woods and three delicate-looking black horses who came and looked at us. When we got back we found a farmer on horseback half way through the front door of the Inn chatting to Mr Crosby. Three lords of the manor with their dogs have arrived today for a week's shooting. Back to Sevenoaks tomorrow.

DECEMBER 10TH

To stay the night at Blackheath with Kenneth [*My brother who was now practising in London.*] It was bitterly cold and K had to go out to a fire watching meeting. This place [*Lindsey House, which had been my first married home, where my children had been born and which, when we moved, had been taken on by my brother*] is full of memories and ghosts. I wrote letters by the fire, not feeling too well and making little effort I fear to talk to K's gentle, ineffectual and tired housekeeper. But when K came in and we settled down after supper he told me he was going to marry again. She is quite young, a physiotherapist who has been working for him. His cheerfulness and the prospect of a new life for him made me experience the first real gladness I had felt for a long time and I went to bed happy in spite of threatening flu.

CHRISTMAS DAY

Jane is unable to get home till early January, but Chris is with us. The morning was spent in trying to get through to speak to Jane on the phone and failing. Then we bicycled to Brasted to church as we don't much care for the services at St Nicholas. Chris was annoyed because his pet plan of a 'demand' call to Jane hadn't come off, H was annoyed that, because as we were waiting for the abortive phone call, he had to hurry on his bike, though he had often hurried far more. I was annoyed with both of them for being annoyed. Chris recovered first! The service was quite nice and the congregation very full and varied. We biked home via Otford which was really too far for H's frame of mind. However after a Christmas dinner of the fine chicken Anthea had sent us things began to cheer up and we had carols with the Joneses, Chris and H accompanying charmingly on violin and flute. Have to go and fire watch at school tomorrow, Boxing Day, and C has to get back to Watford.

DECEMBER 30TH

Up to London to do various jobs but managed to slip into a National Gallery concert and enjoyed Cesar Franck and Rubbra. I sat next to a nice Danish girl in the WAAFS. Tried three restaurants unsuccessfully for food and ended up with a very small piece of terrible sausage pie, served by a waitress who said, 'Oh dear, I've just drunk five bottles of lemonade and I feel like a barrage balloon'. In the evening I went to Otford to supper with Dorothy and Ralph Ivens – there was an old schoolfellow of John's there, only seventeen and had been in the army for a year. Ralph looked very tired and incredibly ragged. He insisted on seeing me down the lane and into the bus. He said he was often too tired to speak what with his duties as air raid warden and his work, but otherwise was all right. A warning went as we waited for the bus but nothing happened. The local paper has published the following statistics: the total number of raids in the district this year is 112 as compared with 401 in 1940.

1944

Managed one good day in the holidays with both C and
J home on leave. We went to Tunbridge Wells and saw
Mrs Wiggs of the Cabbage Patch and a nice funny film
with Will Hay, Claude Hulbert and Ernest Thesiger,
lovely, though the cinema was ice cold. Had tea in the
cinema restaurant where there was a 'tea dansant' going
on and C danced with an unknown girl whom J and I
picked on for him and then with me! I never thought I
would dance again but I enjoyed it thoroughly. Jane
disapproved! The rest of the holidays passed quickly –
sadly we lost our little cat Perkin; he died of kidney
trouble. He had been such a close and loving family
friend for ten years and was easily the most intelligent
cat I have ever known.

JANUARY 18TH
Back to school late because of flu – glad to be back really
and enjoyed trying to help Peggy Bryant (History staff)
with her broadcast on Coke of Norfolk. Had Mary and
Jestyn to lunch to eat the pheasant Madeleine had sent

us. We all enjoyed it but I did wish our little Perkin was here still to enjoy it too. In the evening went to concert at school. Beethoven and a breathless Quartet by young Michael Tippett, which I ought to have enjoyed better than I did. I've had a nice letter from Michael Joseph (the publisher) about 'Cats'. Fairly bad raid the other night.

JANUARY 29TH AND 30TH

Very distressed for poor K. Falk and Mrs Crook whose husbands are prisoners in Japan as Eden has made public terrible disclosures about our prisoners there. C home for the day, he and H and I walking in Knole Park heard the first lark. We saw a Rescue Squad directed by Lady Sackville taking away an incendiary bomb container which had been dropped just outside the big garden gate. This contained 700 bombs. Heard that one had been dropped at school and killed a rabbit! They had also been dropped all up the road from Knole. Mended clothes for C after dinner – he went soon after 10 pm. Am reading C. S. Lewis' *Perilandra* and like it much better than I thought I would, parts are inspiring and beautiful. He is not really good on people but very good always about animals.

FEBRUARY 7TH

To London in spite of a blizzard. No luck with shopping but I saw a notice up about 'Citizen Kane' and decided to forego lunch and see it and found it rewarding. It has an original and fast technique. Bought books in Charing

X Road – the blizzard quite gone over and it was a lovely moonlit night to come home by. London looked beautiful and noble, all its scars hidden and its ugliness gone – its streets peaceful and empty and no lights but the moon.

FEBRUARY 11TH – 14TH

To Devon with H for the weekend to see the parents. Took them to Sidmouth for a lunch. Darling Mother wanted to help the proprietor with the washing up! Felt sad at her marked loss of memory but this doesn't affect her love or her wisdom. She said to me: 'Never forget, everyday you are one more day nearer to the end of the War; you can't help being.' Dad *forceably* read aloud to us sermons from tea to supper time and after supper we had to listen to the BBC service. He had the usual anti-religious effect on me. At 89 he is full of amazing and terrifying vigour, overflowing with plans for going back to Hodcombe, thinking, poor dear, that all will be the same as it was, which of course won't be so, alas.

Home to find three windows broken by a land mine which came down in Knole Park while we were away; very glad to have missed it!

FEBRUARY 19TH

After Famine Relief Committee I caught the midday train to London and waited with growing misery outside the Albert Hall for Chris for nearly three quarters of an hour. At last the poor boy came, having had a foul journey as usual, over 2½ hours from Watford, no heating and no food of course. But we got in all right at the last moment and much enjoyed the concert – Elgar's Introduction for Strings, Metner playing his own new piano Concerto and Beethoven's 8th. Much as I love the National Gallery concerts, I felt all the exhilaration of seeing and hearing a big orchestra play again. I wish I didn't like Beethoven so much the best! C just had time to have a late tea with me in Kensington afterwards.

FEBRUARY 20TH

Friends meeting here; then walked with H to inspect bomb damage at Knole which happily was less than we had been told; wind too cold for comfort. Chris came for the night. We listened to the Brains Trust and I am glad that he doesn't agree with Samuel about the nature of reality. We then did the New Statesman competition, which was to produce a particularly complicated rhyming sonnet. C's was a much better effort than mine – on choosing a hat – rather fun we thought:

'Good morning Modom – no, it is not hot. What
Can I do for you today, pray say?
A hat! Yes, Modom, and in jade, shade made?
We have one here there's been a dash on, fashion's
passion.
Looks charmingly on Modom's fair hair; there!
Or do you favour this with blue? You do
Injustice to your face in that flat hat.
But this cute sailor style in twill will kill.
Yes, Modom, just a trifle daring wearing – squaring
On the head gives better pose – those bows

Are smart indeed, but won't you try my sly
Model here in indigo – no?
It does not please? Now, this is neat, sweet treat
On Modom's head! You'll take the white? Quite right!

Raids each night but hardly minded them at all. H has
been asked to take an additional job for the Admiralty.
I am pleased because he is pleased but I am a bit worried
because of the extra work it entails for him. We listened
in bed to Paul Robeson – really how marvellous radio
is! The Germans have taken over entirely in Italy and I
greatly fear the damage our bombing will do there. The
Italians never wanted to fight anyway. How hateful if *we*
destroy Rome or any of the other lovely cities; already
the monastery of Cassino has been bombarded because
the Germans have occupied it.

FEBRUARY 29TH
Rather a grim but not unhappy day. Not feeling too well
but taught as usual. After tea went to dentist then home
but had to go back to school for fire watching. Just as I
was thinking of getting to bed (this time in the Upper
Staff room) the warning went. I spent half an hour
outside, wearing a very heavy helmet and walking round
the buildings in the company of the warden. All Clear
went about 11 pm but, thinking there would probably
be another raid, I couldn't settle off properly and slept
badly.

MARCH 1ST

Tired, but enjoyed judging the Reading Competition at school today – some of the children read very well indeed, especially the juniors. The whole school listened. Little Barbara Goldsmid read De la Mare's 'Maria Fly' and was *so* unselfconscious and engrossed in it that she seemed totally oblivious of the ordeal and giggled deliciously to herself at the funny parts. Miss Ramsay came to supper to eat our hare and seemed to enjoy it. She and H talked politics amiably. She said she was seriously considering offering me the post of History mistress when Peggy leaves! Of course I shouldn't accept – I have no qualifications for history and anyway it would mean far too much work. You have to *know* things to teach history. Still, I *am* flattered. Very noisy raid at night. I read Beatrix Potter's *The Tailor of Gloucester* aloud to H in bed. He appreciated it just as he should. What perfect prose she writes – I wish I could ground all my pupils on B. Potter and the Authorized Version.

MARCH 3RD

To London to an interview with 'Adprint', the publishing firm for whom I might be doing a children's book on Circuses – really it's the new line in photographic illustrations that they are interested in. Dear Nancy B. came with me. She was at her best, full of life and enjoyment; making me see the beauty of the sun shining through the smoke on the rails at London Bridge which I never thought a beauty-spot before! At Adprint I was faced with a terrifying great man, looking like Beethoven at his fiercest and a long, thin photographer tying himself into coils. There were also some exotic-looking office girls hovering round. My little ideas sounded feeble in front of such an audience and I hated having to trot them out, yet felt pretty sure I could do better than their Zoo book, the script of which made me want to scream, it was so dull. I think that photography is a bad medium for illustrations, especially for children. I am rather bored at having to go to Chessington to look at elephants and circus horses with the photographer – still it doesn't seem as though it can be avoided.

After the interview I met Nancy again for a good meal at the Vega and then we went to the Leicester Galleries to see an exhibition of Fay and Robin's pictures and Frank Dobson's sculpture. Robin's work has become strikingly and rather appallingly like Fay's, only less good. Hers are slashing but nice colours, though I did not like the child with one black cheek and one pink. Frank Dobson's terra cotta figures modern but with classical grace and simplicity were restful after the pictures. I helped Nancy to choose one to buy. She sold her little Bouduin for fifteen guineas in order to do this. It was exciting to buy something at a gallery again.

MARCH 4TH

Had Elfrida (my young niece) to lunch from school. I think she enjoyed it, especially the hare! In the afternoon went to a F.O.R. [*Fellowship of Reconciliation*] meeting feeling a hypocrite as usual because, in this war, I cannot be an out-and-out pacifist. I met a nice Miss Brockle-hurst there who seems in rather a sad way between an incompatible sister and arthritis, poor thing. Corrected

'Free Place' papers in the evening, a job I really hate.
Listened to Schubert with H in bed at night.

MARCH 18TH

A queer day spent at Chessington Zoo with Mr Hinds,
the young photographer whom I like much more than I
thought I would at first. He comes from Street and
is, of course therefore related to the Clark family! At
Chessington we were received by the proprietor, an ex-
Police Sergeant, a huge desolate-looking animal in explo-
sive-looking Harris tweeds, whom we both disliked. The
Ring Master, however, was jovial and friendly and we
watched the elephants practising their tricks. I couldn't
help feeling sorry for the great beasts. The horses were
a much more cheerful sight and one could believe that
they enjoyed their life. We were told that one beautiful
Arab horse was worth about £800. Mr Hinds was very
worried by the lack of atmosphere, the difficulties of
lighting etc. We were given a cup of tea in the panelled
baronial hall and then walked back to the station only
to find it partially closed and no train going for at least
an hour. We managed to get into the waiting room and
I read to him aloud from my Penguin book on the 'Fin
de Siècle', but neither of us found it very interesting so
we got into the empty train and discussed education. I
just missed my train home.

APRIL 21ST

I am enjoying the peace of the holidays and my family
and friends and always H, if only it wasn't for the dark

shadow of the war. I lunched with Elizabeth Buxton today. There was old yellow-eyed Mr Buxton there and someone whom I first took to be a poor refugee as she was in a dingy black coat, a shapeless red knitted dress, no stockings and worn canvas shoes but she turned out to be an intimate friend of General Wingate and a lecturer on engineering at the Imperial Institute. Home, and then on to Blackheath for the night. Kenneth worried about the parents and Dad's determination to go back to Hodcombe as soon as the authorities allow it. I suppose it *is* very isolated for three old people over eighty, though I understand his longing for his beloved home. It will need repairs too, for though the Army have never occupied it, it has been deserted now for over four years.

APRIL 25TH

My birthday. Went to London – Dorothy came to the station to give me a bunch of wallflowers to smell in the train. First met H and went to Bernard Meninsky's exhibition at Peter Jones. Nora Meninsky there – she is quite beautiful, fair with large brown eyes. H wanted to buy me a picture (snow scene) for a birthday present but virtuously I didn't let him and we bought it for a wedding present for K instead. Lunched at the Antelope in Chelsea and walked about looking at houses, many lovely ones for sale at reasonable prices (because of the war). We were tempted by them but don't really want to live in London. Then I took Elfrida to the Circus which was a great success – especially the horses and the sea lion and acrobats.

1944

APRIL 29TH

Kenneth's wedding at St Jude's Church, Golders Green – chief impressions of which were his happy, much younger-looking face, the solid phalanx of elderly sisters (self included) in the front seats, the loud remarks of a baby in the congregation and my new sister-in-law's sense of humour.

WHITSUN, MAY 19TH

Barbara's daughter born, very hot weather. Yesterday I discussed next year's work with Miss Ramsay – it looks as though I shall have a good deal of the VI forms which quite pleases me but I wonder if the best thing would have been to leave at the end of this year while still in a mistaken haze of approval. I'm bound to be found out! Still, I should miss it all now. On Whit Saturday H and I had a good day bicycling and walking all day long. Penshurst was at its best – the river banks thick with forgetmenot and yellow iris – the meadows fragrant. Groombridge was too full of army and there was a good deal of activity in the air.

JUNE 6TH

Invasion of France begun at dawn. So far it has been successful with less loss of life to us than was expected. Great excitement at school – everyone gathered together to listen to the 10 o'clock news. Also it is marvellous that Rome has been evacuated by the Germans with no harm done to the buildings. The weather now is cold and windy which is bad for us.

JUNE 15TH

A horrid day – teaching went badly. I didn't feel well and slept badly as the alert went constantly and there was an incessant noise of low flying planes, machine gun fire and explosions. I thought it was our fighters but I was mistaken.

JUNE 16TH

Discovered that the row last night was from the Germans' new weapon – pilotless planes. Found chaos at school: no one had slept much. It was decided not to send the boarders away for half term and it was given out that no one was to leave the school buildings without permission. Completely by chance my first lesson was 'Julius Caesar' and the first speech to be read was from Act 2 Scene 2:

'Nor heaven nor earth have been at peace tonight.
. . . . Think you to walk forth?
You shall not stir out of your house today.
. . . . Fierce fiery warriors fight upon the clouds
In ranks and quadrons and right forms of war
The noise of battle hurtled in the air.'

The children exclaimed with astonishment and delight at the aptness of the passage. I went on with heartfelt gratitude to Shakespeare who has said everything necessary for every occasion, including the attack of new air weapons:

'Cowards die many times before their death.
The valiant never taste of death but once
Of all the wonders that I yet have heard
It seems to me most strange that men should fear
Seeing that death – a necessary end
Will come when it will come.'

I don't think that class will easily forget that particular
bit of 'Julius Caesar' anyway.

Slept in shelter from 1.30 am not very well. Sleeping
under the Morrison shelter is very oppressive. [*The Morrison shelter (named after Herbert Morrison the Labour
M.P.) was designed for indoor use. It was like a very heavy
table clamped to the floor.*]

JUNE 19TH AND 20TH

Raids continued all day and all night very noisy, but not
very frightening. I rearranged our sleeping quarters and
gardened. The white kitten Sandro, who has now been
with us a fortnight, is still rather wild and scratchy, but
seems quite good about birds so far and may not be too
unworthy a successor to Perkin.

JUNE 30TH

Raids have been going on pretty continuously. It is very
tiring at school and difficult teaching underground in
the stuffy dark trenches crouched on the wire bunks. A
good many of the children have now been sent away to
safer districts. The poor School Certificate and Higher
Certificate candidates had to do their exam papers either

in the trenches or, if in the classrooms, to get down under their desk tables each time a bomb came over – sometimes five times in one paper! I was invigilating for an art exam when the form had to disappear several times beneath the desks and I saw one arm after another stretch out and up, grab their paper and paint brush and continue on the ground.

The continual spotting duty is very trying – air raid warnings are often too late for doodle bugs and so a member of the staff is always outside in the grounds on guard. It is anxious work, especially when there is a high wind, for what with that and our own aircraft it is hard to distinguish sounds. I gave the alarm the other morning and everyone rushed for shelter and it turned out only to be the motor mower on the recreation grounds nearby!

The whole of June has been a month of deep, grey gloom and oppression. At school the staff are getting worn out and short-tempered; poor Miss Ramsay, responsible for all those children, is noticeably and understandably so. There have been only three fine days in the whole month, none of which I wasted I am glad to say for on one I biked to lovely Penshurst, on another walked to Magpie Bottom and on the third I had tea with Mary and the babies in the garden. The consistent bad weather has been the best possible for the doodle bugs and the worst for our invasion operations.

JULY 1ST – 9TH
Managed to make 15 lbs of strawberry jam from strawberries picked at Halstead. The weekends just about keep me sane; Chris home this one for three scattered

nights. He sleeps under the dining room table – he was tired, rather depressed at first but soon became quite jovial. I dreamed last night that I was in a London bus and had just said to H, 'I hope a doodle bug doesn't catch us here,' when I woke to a great crash – our skylight window gone again. The Cummingses rang up in great agitation as they had heard it was in Six Bells Lane opposite us. Broughton Manor at Otford I fear is badly damaged. The cats are a great comfort through all this – little black Vicky and little white Sandro, leaping about the garden and playing with their tails.

JULY 10TH

At midday at school the alarm went and everyone in the Staff room went out and sat on the ground in the passage with their backs against the wall (which is supposed to be safer than remaining upright in the room!). We heard the sound of the doodle bug cut out just overhead (which meant it was coming down) and no one spoke for a very long minute or two but it must have been a dud or I wouldn't be writing this now. I didn't feel fear, just a suspension of all feeling and a sense of timelessness.

JULY 27TH

To Whimple for the weekend to see the parents and our two evacuee schoolchildren who are billeted at Ottery St Mary. I found them homesick and eager for news of school. I took them to church on Sunday morning. It was the first time they had been to a Church of England service, being strict little Nonconformists, and they didn't think much of it I'm afraid, in fact they were rather shocked at its ritual, candles etc. I also interviewed the headmaster of the school they were attending who inhabits a very untidy and rather dirty room, but has an extremely firm and cultured secretary. They seem to be settling in all right.

Usual heartache about Mother's memory. Stopped off on the way home to see Madeleine who as ever, gave me lovely food. Rob very charming and knowledgeable about trees and flowers. He brought me a picture book of German aircraft to look at and when I said I did not care for that sort of book he replied kindly, 'No, I expect it's a little too German for you Granny.'

JULY 31ST

Broke up, thankful to see the last of this trying term. We had a school meeting on the front lawn – about seventy children are left, the others scattered over the country as evacuees. A flying bomb came over just as Miss Ramsay began her speech and everyone vanished like rabbits underground. When we re-assembled Miss Ramsay continued undaunted from where she had left off. We had one more disturbance and then were left in peace. Classes have been reduced to about one third, I finished 'Julius Caesar' in the teeth of raids and trench teaching with no books, but R remarked, 'I am so sorry we've finished it, I've liked doing it so much,' which was nice.

1944

FIRST WEEK IN AUGUST

The holidays have begun well with Jane at home on leave. We have seen 'This Happy Breed' and 'La Femme de Boulanger', together, both very good films – also enjoyed a reading of Pope at the Poetry Society meeting at the Ashbees. But perhaps the best day was with H on Saturday when we went bicycling to the Kent and Sussex borders and to see the old farmhouse Pickdock, which belongs to Ellen's cousin. We travelled leisurely with our bikes to Winchelsea in the luggage van, eating our lunch sitting on boxes and then took to the road. The farmhouse, empty now, looked perfect – the wood and the oast houses sheltering it so comfortably and a blue distant line of sea at the end of the long garden. A bomb passed very low and exploded over the wood and on our journey back we noticed a good deal of damage to farms and cottages. While we waited at Winchelsea Station, looking at the lovely countryside, we saw two bombs shot down in ten minutes and another from the train. It seemed quite unreal, like a film, shown on the screen of the sky to entertain us while we waited.

3RD WEEK IN AUGUST

At Cheltenham. Elizabeth's friend, Miss Tetley, staying here; when she was headmistress of a school of 600 girls she got the maximum salary then of £120 p.a. News begins to be exciting – things at last are moving fast in Normandy. [*The victory at Falaise which opened the way to Paris.*] I went on to Abingdon, dear Northcourt House was much more cheerful with no nurse or elderly invalids about and Mrs Tatham seemed very well and very much herself. Rose, who used to be housemaid when I was at Oxford, had come back and asked me how I could manage to leave my babies. I said they would be 21 years old this autumn! Evelyn was happy and the only drawback was the food which was ghastly. Sylvia is completely defeatist over it and it was mostly dried eggs, bacon and pilchards, cold coffee, terrible cocoa and badly cooked vegetables. She was charming and interesting however about a lecture she was giving on 'Values in English Literature'. The news was so good we all got very excited about it. E and I talked a great deal up in the old schoolroom and played paper games with each other, getting exactly the same score and went to see Roger Livesey in 'The Banbury Nose' which was good.

AUGUST 23RD

Paris liberated by the French! Went to London and lunched with Richard Naish – then to Adprints to see the photographs for the circus book which were very disappointing from the point of view of the script; I got the price up to 30 guineas however.

AUGUST 25TH

Fire watching at school, which has been badly damaged by a flying bomb last week. Very dismal in the empty desolate building full of broken glass and splintered wood. Miss Ramsay arrived very late, tired and worried, but fairly cheerful all the same. We drank hot milk together and then I slept on a camp bed in the Reception Room.

Am very sad that Mrs Barker and 'Uncle' and George the spaniel, have all been killed by a direct hit at Shoreham; the dear old cottage, where Mother and Dad stayed after her operation and where we four also stayed between moves, is now completely destroyed. Mrs Barker did not usually take in people but Dad got round her and she was always so amusing and kind. It was such a pretty peaceful place with its big cottage garden.

On my second night's fire watching I was joined by Daphne Russell about whom I am worried as she seems on the point of a breakdown. She has had no proper holiday and far too much bomb worry. I have brought her home for two nights and am arranging for her to go on to Peggy's.

SEPTEMBER

Off with H for our holiday in Cornwall. Nancy (Cummings) has joined the WRNS and is stationed at Falmouth and she has got us rooms at St Mawes. We travelled by night – a full carriage but I luckily got a corner seat, a soldier put his head on my shoulder and went to sleep. It was a calm night and we saw a moon rainbow; I had never seen one before – most beautiful. The other occupants of our carriage bearable except for one contemptuous naval officer who was rather a trial. No one but us ate anything! At Truro, H, shifting the luggage, dropped a heavy suitcase on my head which stunned me rather, he was very contrite. At Falmouth we got a cup of coffee and the ferry trip to St Mawes freshened me up no end.

St Mawes is almost an island – all the inhabitants have

boats and the children manage them with great skill; there are all sorts of craft about from the historic blue and white invasion barges to the little many-coloured sailing boats that skim over the green water like brilliant butterflies.

SEPTEMBER 5TH

Went to Falmouth to meet Nancy for lunch. She looked most attractive in her uniform and was very amusing about the WRNS. There was a high wind and the waves were splendid. Yesterday we went to St Just to church – strange Saints are thick on the ground in Cornwall. The old clergyman read the prayers as if he was ticking off a store's order.

Our guest house is comfortable and it is bliss to get away from the bombs and sleep in peace. I am reading *Daniel Deronda* again with much pleasure. I had forgotten how very good all the first part about Gwendoline is – painfully good.

SEPTEMBER 6TH

Long walk with Nancy – we discussed our ideal heaven in which for both of us laziness played a big part. The view on the way to Percuil was most lovely – deep green water, pale golden distant hills and in the foreground a solitary scarlet boat and orange corn stooks. Talked in the evening to an interesting woman, an entymologist who has read Gibbons' *Decline & Fall* right through four times!

1944

SEPTEMBER 14TH

Our last day, a wet sea mist but ignoring this we took our usual ferry boat. Sky and headlands shadowy and soft grey. Walked to our special beach in pouring rain and hesitated about bathing but just as we had decided against, it cleared a little and down the cliff we went towards a ghostly sea. We bathed naked as the beach was quite deserted; the sea was warm and the rain had stopped. Afterwards, full of virtue and power we walked to Mrs Ward's farmhouse and had a marvellous meal. On the way home via Portscatho we met our apple lady who went back with us to let us have the last picking.

SEPTEMBER 15TH

Home. Started with lovely rough ferry ride to Falmouth then a tedious but not impossible journey, though we only had 1½ seats between us from Plymouth. Hellish black scenes at Paddington but home by 8.30, eleven hours altogether – the journey down took fifteen hours. Little cats very pleased to see us and looked fine.

SEPTEMBER 16TH – OCTOBER 12TH

Nearly a month has gone by of pleasant, interesting, personal life of teaching, writing papers for the British Council and seeing my friends. Chris came home for one weekend and I enjoyed one afternoon in London with him seeing the historic French film, 'Le Journal de Resistance', *but* the news has not been good during this period. Arnhem was a tragic hold-up and may mean disaster for Holland; the weather has been foully against us all the summer, the Nazis obviously intend to resist to the last man and the war may drag on and on. Before Christmas Chris is probably going to be sent to India where the Japs are on the Burmese frontier.

Now I am waiting for the children to come home for a brief lovely spell to celebrate their 21st birthday. Matty has just finished icing their cake and I have done the flowers and there are piles of letters and parcels waiting for them.

OCTOBER 13TH

Birthday family lunch party in H's room at the Research Department. C and J at the head of the table. I apologized for not having a birthday present for them – C said 'You have given us 21 happy years.' The four of us went to the ballet afterwards.

We are having another family party at home at the weekend to which Madeleine is coming.

NOVEMBER 8TH

Very sad at hearing from Margaret Harvey that she cannot come on Saturday because her sister-in-law had been killed by a flying bomb in Croydon. They were Crosfields (Quakers) and such good, happy, useful people.

Am writing a paper on the English Village for the British Council which is comforting and interesting work.

Chris came home for the day, bringing two WAAFs with him. I liked one of them very much – they went back together but he stayed the night. I said, 'Why do you go about with them in pairs?' He grinned and said, 'I find it safer that way.' H was away doing air raid duty so C stayed chatting to me in bed till I turned him out at midnight. He seems to get on well with his C.O. who is a great character, so C says – a friend of Siegfried Sassoon, writes poetry and hates the war as much as C does.

DECEMBER 10TH

Went to Tunbridge Wells to do Christmas shopping and I am afraid fell for an early edition of *Lambarde's Perambulation in Kent* (1596) for myself. I got this at Hall's bookshop. It was extravagant of me but Mr Pratley says I needn't pay for it yet. I knew him first as assistant to Mr Hall who started this famous shop (in the year I was born); now he owns the shop and is such a nice and knowledgeable man. He told me he simply could not and would not read any author he respected printed on this dreadful war paper.

In the evening I met H at Tonbridge for a lovely concert: Esther Salaman singing folk songs and Vivaldi and Bach conducted by young Tippett.

DECEMBER 24TH – 31ST

War news very depressing; the Germans are advancing again into Belgium and there is civil war in Greece (probably owing to us). Anthea and Gordon and two babies here for Christmas, she very good-tempered and plucky. I enjoyed the children except in the early mornings.

1944

Nicky is very interested in animals, Anna is a placid good infant. The twins couldn't get home but will come in January. Chris thinks he will be off to India early in the New Year.

1945

JANUARY 7TH

Very cold, snow in the afternoon. Children here for their Christmas break and we had a hilarious time all doing the New Statesman competition of a proposal of marriage by telegram. The Joneses came in to supper and carols which we sang much better than at Christmas. Tried not to think of C's going to India in two weeks' time.

JANUARY 17TH

Started school again with a nice VI form and it is satisfactorily fixed up that Jane will teach art there one day a week for this term.

In the evening met C in London. He wanted to take me out for a special treat. We had a meal at the Chinese Restaurant and then went to see 'The Magistrate'.

JANUARY 18TH

Said goodbye to Chris, broke down a bit at parting but not for long and there is a faint chance that he may be able to come home again for one more night. Mary came in the morning to cheer me up and J came back before lunch. At 5.30 home came Chris again and I immediately felt quite light-hearted and able to live in the present and he was much less preoccupied than for weeks. We had a good meal scratched up at the last moment, mostly out of tins and settled in for a long evening and H came back in good time. First we listened to Handel and then C chose Dutch and French pictures out of my postcard collection to take with him and we looked at them together. Then we played our family paper games and altogether it was a perfect evening to remember.

JANUARY 19TH

C and J squabbling over the bathroom like old times. We caught the 10.45 train to London and said goodbye to C in the Charing Cross Road – grey, dirty day and I felt dead and cold. Went to Adprints and British Council Offices. They want me to do a paper for them on 'English Personalities' which will be fun. I shall do Dr Johnson and Cobbett for two anyway and Sir Thomas More and Charles Lamb, I think.

FEBRUARY

C's letters began coming after a gap of only two weeks and he is well and happy and interested in everything. J at home painting and seems to like her teaching alright. I have enjoyed finishing Shakespeare and beginning 'English Personalities' for the British Council and have tried to do a little social work besides school, consisting of sending off parcels to France and supporting F.O.R.,

but not nearly enough and not very well. Various people
here to stay including Madeleine and little Rob. Rockets
have sometimes been tiresome but no nearly so bad as
the flying bombs. The worst moment was when we heard
one had fallen on the Herb Farm next door to the Jones'
new home but it didn't do much damage.

MARCH 19TH

I went to the St Matthew's Passion at the Albert Hall
for the first time. Kathleen Ferrier sang so beautifully.
I liked her the best of all. It was a great experience. I
was alone but saw several people I knew in the interval.

APRIL 13TH

Happy three days with H staying at Tenterden – country
heavenly with blossom of all sorts. Met a Mrs S at the
guest house who had lived at that lovely house Windsors
at Rolvenden Layne which she had just sold for £8,000.
She was helpless, beautiful, sweet and bewildered in a
world which was no longer at her feet. We went over to
Walkhurst to discuss its possible vacancy when the war
ends. Saddened by news of Roosevelt's death. At home
a phone call from Kenneth asking that Chris should be
godfather to his new son, Timothy.

A letter from C arrived today from Cawnpore in which
he says:

'I have just been listening to the news but it has ceased
to thrill me – the more one thinks the war is over the
more slaughter goes on. I find I am becoming more

and more pacifist again, possibly under the influence of Gandhi, of whom I read daily in the papers here.'

APRIL 22ND

Timothy's christening at Blackheath – C godfather by proxy. The old wisteria at Lindsey House is at its best, all was peaceful; one can hardly believe that the rockets and the bombs have really ceased. The papers are full of tales of liberated prisoners and the unspeakable horrors of the concentration camps.

MAY 13TH

Victory Sunday. I had managed to get to a little F.O.R. service yesterday. Mr B spoke on St Paul's theme, that what we want to do we don't do and what we don't want to do we do and that only the power of God can save us. Today I listened to the service of thanksgiving from St Paul's attended by all the royalties and politicians. I missed William Temple very much and chiefly remember the music and Dean Matthews reading 'Whatsoever things are true' etc. and the bells pealing out triumphantly after having been silenced for so long. Letter from C. 'So it seems that I shall be celebrating V-day in Cawnpore. It has come so slowly and painfully and long overdue that the news that we may expect the final surrender in another day or two was hardly any thrill in fact the really exciting news here was the capture of Rangoon. Now I *do* think Japan will pack up fairly soon, everything seems to be pointing that way i.e. I don't think she'll fight to the bitter end like Germany, although we've a long way to go yet.'

JULY 27TH

My production of 'The Critic' at school a success. The children acted really well and looked like a painting by Chardin. E was staying with me and enjoyed it, so did H.

AUGUST 6TH

Atomic bomb dropped on Japan. Felt appalled and miserable.

AUGUST 15TH

Japan has accepted the armistice terms. In the evening I went out with H to see our town rejoice at the end of the war. It was a lovely clear night and Sevenoaks looked very pretty. Festoons of coloured lights met at the Fountain, Martin and Doulton was lit up and so were many other shops. Coloured lights were suspended all round the Vine Recreation ground and the Queen Anne House facing the cricket pitch was floodlit. After the darkness of years this all looked astounding. They were letting off fireworks and the trees (my favourite pines on the way to school) were lit up with a golden and pink light. Crowds of children were making merry, climbing over the cricket marking boards etc. What a contrast to this time last summer! The next day we took the 7 pm train to town. We walked into Trafalgar Square where hundreds of people were collected, swarming all over the lions, perched on the posts like statues, paddling in the pools. A band was playing, a small boy standing on one of the lions' backs and beating time solemnly, people dancing and lots of children around. Everyone happy and good-tempered, no rowdiness. We decided to walk down Whitehall; at Westminster crowds were gathered outside the Houses of Parliament. We strolled down, through the gardens at the back of the Abbey to the river; the grass had grown high, the hedges were unclipped and there were piles of rubble about. The great Towers rose out of this rough country wildness looking as if they really were William Morris's Dung Market in his *News from Nowhere*. No one but ourselves were here; the lights began to gleam out across the water and a slight rain to fall. We wandered round the Abbey cloisters and the little courts, a sentimental journey in the gathering dusk. Then we rejoined the crowds and boarded a bus and leaned out of the window upstairs waving to the cheering, laughing people as our bus got mixed up with all the MPs who were just leaving the House. We got off the bus at Waterloo Bridge and walked across. Somerset House, Westminster and St Paul's were lit up – all safe now. Filled with love of London, we walked along the Strand and down again to the Embankment, climbing over piles of fallen masonry and then a wild rush through crowds and rain to catch our train home at Charing Cross. The day after, we started off for our summer break with our trusty bikes to Stair in the Lake District. It was while we were there that my father, now in his ninety-first year, read the lesson in a BBC evening service. We sat by the open

window of our farmhouse lodging sitting room and listened; his voice came over the air as clear and resonant
and confident as ever. He read from the Apocrypha, the
story of Shadrach Mesach and Abednego: 'Then from
the *midst of the fire* Abednego stood and prayed, "Thou
O Lord art worthy to be praised".'

Beyond the dark valley the distant mountains were
glowing with light and as we watched the glow deepen
the words came ringing out triumphantly:

'O ye mountains and hills praise the Lord
Praise and exalt Him above all forever.'